THE PEOPLE OF
OLD MACHAR
&
OLD TOUN ABERDEEN
1696

taken from
List of Pollable Persons in the Shires of Aberdeen
1696

Volume 2

The Book or List off Pollable persons within the Shire off **Aberdein** & Burgh within the same

Containing the names off the haill persones poleable and Polemoney payable be them conforme to their respective capacities According to the Act off Parliament anent Polemoney daited the   day of

Faithfullie extracted ffurth of the Princpall Lists off poleable persones off each paroch within the Shyre as they were reported by the Comissioners and Clerks for the severall paroches appointed ffor that effect

By **William Hay** Collector appointed off the polemoney payable ffurth of the said shire

And revised and examined by ane Quorum of the **Commissioners** of Supplie off the samen Shyre and attested by them the first day of Aprile 1696.

This Book belongs to Thomas Gordon of Buthlaw

The title page from the 'List of Pollable Persons'.

INTRODUCTION

During the late seventeenth century the Scottish economy cupboard was bare and the need for extra revenue was essential. One of the ways used was a tax on people- A POLL TAX - and several were collected during the 1690's. Supposedly a tax on every person over the age of sixteen not a beggar, although this has been disputed. Therefore for genealogical purposes an extant list of over 30,000 names from 1696 is of immense value. Even more so is the transcription and publication, in two volumes, of this unique document by the Gentlemen of the County in 1844. It is from this edition that our facsimile reprint comes, also included is two pages from the original 1696 volume.

Anyone wishing to check the original will find it in Aberdeen University Archives (MS548). Our thanks must go to the staff of both the Archives and Special Collections departments of the University Library for their help. The two photographs of the original are reproduced by kind permission of the Archives. Although dated 1696 the date the lists were approved, in fact they were compiled in September 1695.

A history of the original volume is also interesting - it was in the library of Thomas Gordon of Buthlaw and his descendants till their fortunes failed and the estate was sold during the First World War. The book was then bought by Col. D.F.Davidson who donated it to Aberdeen University in the 1920's.

In the Special Collections department of the University (housed in the same building as the Archives) there exists an Index to the 'List' compiled in the 19th century by Dingwall Fordyce, however it is a very selective list consisting only of the more 'important' people. The index included here is comprehensive and also includes a place name index as well as an occupation breakdown.

Several points have to be made to make understanding this volume easier:
1) Any errors in the 1844 published version have been perpetuated in this edition.
2) The original page numbers of the 1844 edition have been used throughout.
3) The following places have not been located on the maps - ATHRENCROFT, CAIRNSLUM, CARNOUSTIE, MILNBOGG, WOODEND.

LESLEY DIACK.

VIII. PRESBYTRIE OF ABERDEEN.

AN LIST of the POLABLE PERSONS within the PARIOCHIN of OLD MACHAR, excepting the Freedome Lands of Aberdeen, given up be Mr. JAMES GRAY *of Balgounie and* JAMES GORDONE *of Seatoune, two Commissioners nominate and appointed for that effect, and be Mr.* JOHN ROBERTSONE, *Clerk and Collector appointed be them for the said Pariochin.*

THE WALUED RENT of the said pariochin is £5747 7 10
    Proportionat among the heritors thus:—

Imprimis, Mr. James Gray of Balgounie	£720	0	0
Toun of Old Aberdeen	650	0	0
George Paton of Grandhom	600	0	0
Toun of Aberdeen, for Gilcomstone	501	1	2
Toun of Aberdeen, for Ruthrestown	300	0	0
James Gordon, for his Lands	266	13	4
Item, for half nets fishing upon Don	166	13	4
Mr. Alexander Davidson, for Berrihill, and his fishing	400	0	0
Earle of Panmuire	300	0	0
Mr. Patrick Sandelands of Cotton	293	6	8
Laird of Hiltown	283	6	8
Mr. Andrew Massie, for his fishing upon Don	200	0	0
Relict of Mr. William Moir	200	0	0
Mr. John Gordon, for half nets fishing upon Don	166	13	4
Relict of Mr. William Johnston	166	13	4
Doctor Mores relict	150	0	0
Mr. George Peacok, for Pitmuxton	120	0	0
John Lesslie, for Whytestrypes	110	0	0
Andrew Cassie, for his oun and B. Blacks Land	58	0	0
William Robertsone, for Peterstone	50	0	0
Heirs of John Moir, for Sunisyde	45	0	0
		5747	7 10

Mr. JAMES GRAY of Balgounie his lands of valued rent is £720 0 0

The hundred pairt, payable be the tennents, is £7 4 0

Imprimis, Alexander Still in Murcar is	£0	14	0
Alexander Gibson ther, is	0	14	0
John Gray ther, is	0	8	4
Alexander Still, younger ther	0	8	4
John Bodie ther	0	8	4
Robert Gray ther	0	8	4
Thomas Still in Wastfield	0	6	8
Richard Drum in Cairnfield	0	6	4
	£3	14	4

10. PAROCH OF OLD MACHAR.

(The rest of the lands being possest be the said heritor, the proportione of the walued rent payable be himself is £3 9s. 8d., but being polable in a higher capacity, is not layable.)

Balgounes Family.

His valued rent being as said is £720, he is of poll with the generall poll	£12	6	0
Margaret Menzies, his lady, her poll is	0	6	0
Item, two sons, John and James, their poll, with the generall poll, is	3	12	0
Item, two daughters *in familia*, their poll is	0	12	0
Mr. Alexander Hatt, servant, fee 40 merks, the fortieth pairt and generall poll,	0	19	4
William Josse, 32 merks per annum, the fortieth pairt and generall poll is	0	16	8
Alexander Gill, his servant, of fee 26 merks, the fortieth part and generall poll,	0	14	8
John Gray, his servant, 35 merks per annum, fortieth pairt and generall poll	0	17	8
Adam Watson, £20 per annum, the fortieth pairt and generall poll is	0	16	0
John Blair, £20 per annum, the fortieth pairt and generall poll is	0	16	0
George Brow, 32 merks per annum, the fortieth pairt and generall poll is	0	16	8
William Andersone, £24 per annum, the fortieth pairt and generall poll	0	18	0
Andrew Robertsone, 16 merks per annum, the fortieth pairt and generall poll is	0	11	4
George Tillery, 32 merks per annum, the fortieth part and generall poll is	0	16	8
Isobell Mundy, £40 per annum, the fortieth pairt and generall poll is	1	6	0
Isobell Ritchie, 14 merks per annum, the fortieth part and generall poll is	0	10	8
Margarat Couper, Christian Watson, and Margarat Findlay, each £10 per annum, the fortieth part and generall poll is	1	13	0
	£28	8	8

Tennents of Balgounie in Murcar.

Alexander Still, elder, fermer, and Christane Watsone, his wife, generall poll	£0	12	0
Alexander Darg, servant, fee £18, fortieth part and generall poll is	0	15	0
John Mitchell, servant, his fee 22 merks, fortieth part and generall poll is	0	13	4
Alexander Still, fee £8, fortieth pairt and generall poll	0	10	0
James Christell, fee 5 merks, fortieth part and generall poll is	0	7	8
Anna Frost, fee £8, fortieth part and generall poll is	0	10	0
George Litlejohn, wyver and grassman, for trade and generall poll	0	12	0
William Litlejohn, grassman and wyver, for trade and generall poll	0	12	0
Elspeth Josse, his mother, *in familia*	0	6	0
John Mill, grassman and wyver, and Margaret Walker, his spouse poll is	0	18	0
Jean Mill, daughter *in familia*, poll is	0	6	0
Jean Still, spouse to the forsaid Alexander Darg, her poll is	0	6	0
ALEXANDER GIBSONE, tennent, and his spouse, with their generall poll	0	12	0
William Symmer, servant, 28 merks fee, and generall poll	0	15	4
John Tillery, servant, £8 per annum, fortieth pairt and generall poll is	0	10	0
Alexander Adam, £8, the fortieth pairt and generall poll	0	10	0
Isobell Still, 14 merks, the fortieth pairt and generall poll	0	10	8
Jean Thain, £8 per annum, the fortieth pairt and generall poll is	0	10	8
Margarat M'Kain and Margarat Andersone, grasswomen, of generall poll	0	12	0
John Gray, tennent (no trade nor stock), for generall poll is	0	6	0
Agnes Thomsone, his spouse (no children), her generall poll	0	6	0

VIII. PRESBYTRIE OF ABERDEEN.

Alexander Still, younger, tennent, and his wyfe, their poll is..........................	£0	12	0
James Bodie, tennent, and Elizabeth Watt, his spouse (no children, no servants)	0	12	0
Margarat Frost, his servant, £4, fortieth part and generall poll	0	8	0
Robert Gray, farmer, and Isobell Gray, his wyfe, poll.................................	0	12	0
Agnes Wright, servant, fee £7, the fortieth pairt and generall poll	0	9	6
ALEXANDER LESLIE, tennent ther (no trade or stock), his poll is..................	0	6	0
Janet Knight, his wife, her generall poll is...	0	6	0
Alexander Paull ther (no trade, no stock), his own and his wifes generall poll is..	0	12	0
Alexander Yett, servant, £8 per annum, fortieth pairt and generall poll	0	10	0
ROBERT GIBSONE, tennent ther, his generall poll is	0	6	0
Isobell Keith, his wife, poll is...	0	6	0
Jean Gibson, their daughter, *in familia*, poll is	0	6	0
James Hendersone ther, no trade or stock, his poll is	0	6	0
Jannet Hendersone, his daughter, her poll is	0	6	0
Christian Hendersone, spous to the said John Gray, servitrix to the Laird of Balgounie, they have no children of age, servants, or stock, her poll is	0	6	0
James Christell and Elizabeth Leed, pensioners	0	0	0
	£17	3	6

SILVERBURNE.

James Steven ther, no trade, his generall poll is......................................	£0	6	0
Isobell Gill, his spouse, his generall poll is	0	6	0
James Stott, servant, fee 20s. per annum, the fortieth part and poll is	0	6	0
Alexander Gill ther, and Isobell Still, his spouse, their poll........................	0	12	0
Alexander Elrick, glower, and his spouse, their poll is................................	0	18	0
John Ritchie ther, and his wyfe and son, John, *in familia*, their poll is............	0	18	0
Barbara Walker, servant, fee 8 merks, fortieth pairt and generall poll............	0	8	8
John Watt, smith ther, and his wyfe, their poll is (no children of age).............	0	18	0
	£4	13	2

BALGOUNIE.

William Gray (no trade or free stock), and wyfe, their poll..........................	£0	12	0
Margarat Ferguson, servant, fee £8, fortieth pairt and generall poll is..............	0	10	0
George Proctor (no trade or free stock), and Christian Steinsone, his spouse (no children of age, no servants or subtennents) their generall poll is......	0	12	0
John Laurenstone, wyver, and his wyfe, their poll is.......................................	0	18	0
Bessie Steven, servant, fee £8 per annum, the fortieth pairt and generall poll...	0	10	0
George Meassone, and his wyfe (no trade or stock), ther generall poll is..........	0	12	0
John Fergusone, shoemaker, and his wyfe (no children or servants), their poll is	0	18	0
William Booth, shoemaker, and Jean Innes, his spouse, and four children of age, James, Jean, Christian, and Agnes, their poll is......................	2	2	0
Margarat Leslie, relict of John Umphrey, workman, her generall poll is.........	0	6	0
Jean Umphray, her daughter *in familia*, her generall poll............................	0	6	0
Margaret Jacksone, spouse to William Andersone, servitor to the Laird of Balgounie, her poll is..	0	6	0
Agnes Shand, spouse to Andrew Robertsone, servitor to the Laird of Balgounie, her poll is...	0	6	0

10. PAROCH OF OLD MACHAR.

Alexander Proctor, flesher, and Bessie Brodie, his spouse, with a daughter of age, called Jean, their poll is...	£1	4	0
Jannet Messon, servant, fee £8, fortieth pairt and generall poll.....................	0	10	0
Margarat Chyne, the like fee and poll..	0	10	0
Robert Sclait, shoemaker, and Marjorie Smith, his spouse, their poll is...........	0	18	0
Christian Frasser, spous to John Blair, servitor to the Laird of Balgoune, her generall poll is..	0	6	0
Elizabeth Gerard and Isobell Dyce, pensioners...	0	0	0
	£11	6	0

WESTFIELD.

Thomas Still (no trade or free stock), and Isobell Clerk, his spous, their poll...	£0	12	0
Janet Still, their daughter *in familia*, her poll is......................................	0	6	0
William Murray ther (no trade), with his wyfe, their generall poll..................	0	12	0
Margaret Watt, servant (no fee), her poll is...	0	6	0
	£1	16	0

CAIRNFIELD.

Alexander Christell (no trade), and Jannet Symer, his spouse, their poll.........	£0	12	0
Richard Drum (no trade), and Bessie Cairngill, his spouse, their poll............	0	12	0
Alexander Finnie, gardner, and Elizabeth Grig, his spouse, her poll is.........	0	18	0
Patrick Gray, and his wyfe (no free stock, &c.), their generall poll is.............	0	12	0
James Litlejohn, his father-in-law *in familia*, his poll is............................	0	6	0
Elizabeth Beverly, fee 10 merks, fortieth pairt and generall poll	0	9	4
John Innes, wyver, and Elizabeth Christell, his wyfe (no stock, &c.), with on daughter, Jean, *in familia*, their generall poll...	1	4	0
	£4	13	4

CATHOK MILL.

Thomas Hector (no trade), and Margarat Strachan, his wyfe, their poll is........	£0	12	0
John Mill, servant (no fee), his generall poll...	0	6	
Margaret Syme, fee 13 merks, the fortieth pairt and generall poll is...............	0	10	4
Christian Watsone ther, her generall poll...	0	6	0
John Barron, wakster, and Margarat Davidsone, his spouse, their poll is.........	0	18	0
Margaret Black, servant, fee £8, fortieth pairt and generall poll.....................	0	10	0
	£3	2	4

TOWN OF OLD ABERDEEN.

The said toun is two hundred and eighteen bolls of beer or great oats showing, valued to six hundred and fifty pound of yearly rent......................	£650	0	0

On heritor being possessor hereof would be subject and layable of £12 of poll, but in regaird by twenty-seven several heritors, whereof the Kings Colledge is on, and hes 60 bolls, bought with mortified money for burses; the Hospitall of Old Aberdeen is another, and hes 17½ bolls for the bidemen; Christain Huisone hes 20 bolls, and polled in New Aberdeen; Mr. James Londie, minister at North Leith, 16 bolls; Jean Thow 12 bolls, and polled in Aberdeen; Heirs of Thomas Shand of Craig, 9 bolls, and polled in a higher capacity in the paroch of Dyce, being in all 134 bolls, 2 firlots. The other 83½ bolls showing

VIII. PRESBYTRIE OF ABERDEEN.

is divided amongst twenty-one severall heritors, the greatest of which will not exceed 7 bolls showing, and so by Act of Parliament will not be layable, as not being £20 Scots of valued rent. However its left to the judges competent to determine.

The TOUN of OLD ABERDEEN being of valued rent.................................. £650 0 0

The hundreth pairt whereof in name of poll is................................... .... £6 10 0

Proportionat among the tennents thus:—

Imprimis, John Kinnaird...	£0	1	4
Alexander Sangster	0	2	8
Alexander Mathewson	0	1	0
Alexander Glass..	0	2	0
James Mill..	0	1	4
John Nicol	0	4	10
Gilbert Broun...	0	5	0
John Melvell...	0	1	0
George Cushney	0	1	4
George Mill...	0	5	4
Alexander Christie..	0	6	0
John Bannerman	0	3	4
George Ronald..	0	2	8
William Mackie...	0	2	8
William Jeans...	0	2	0
John Chalmer..	0	3	4
Alexander Strachan	0	5	0
Duncan Cassie..	0	2	8
Peter Cheynes relict...	0	3	4
George Taylor...	0	5	4
George Allan	0	1	4
George Henderson..	0	2	8
Jannet Moir...	0	4	8
Peter Fraser	0	4	8
James Thomsone...	0	3	0
William Baxter..	0	3	4
Margarat Couper...	0	3	0
William Wilsone	0	1	4
James Marnoch	0	2	8
James Fiddes..	0	10	8
William Sangster	0	2	8
John Auld	0	2	0
Margaret Lind...	0	0	8
Lucres Glennie	0	3	4
James Jaffray	0	0	8
James Messone	0	2	0

10. PAROCH OF OLD MACHAR.

John Bodweel	£0	3	4			
Andrew Baxter	0	4	0			
				£5	14	6

The balance of the proportione wanting is 15s. 6d., and payable be Dr. George Midletone, and Dr. Garden, and Mr. Alexander Fraser, regent, John Peddor in Aberdeen, Andrew Cassie in Old Aberdeen, Anna Duncan, relict of Mr. Robert Forbes, Alexander Gordon, younger, in Old Aberdeen, but they, being polled in higher capacityes, are not layable. They are all polled in Old Aberdeen, except John Pedder and Alexander Sangster, who are polled in the city of New Aberdeen.

GEORGE PATTON OF GRANDHOM.

The said GEORGE PATTON his lands of valued rent is	£600	0	0
The hundred pairt, payable in name of poll	£6	0	0
Proportionat thus amongst the tennents:—			
Imprimis, George Bartlet, younger, in Grandhom	£0	14	0
Alexander Walker at the Mill of Grandhom	0	3	0
Peter Ritchie in Denstoun	0	10	0
David Hill ther	0	10	0
Thomas Watt in Persley	0	10	0
James Still ther	0	10	0
John Fettes ther	0	10	0
William Thomsone ther	0	3	0
Alexander Watsone in Brigetoune	0	8	0
Andrew Sangster in Buckie	0	8	0
George Bartlet, elder, ther	0	8	0
David Andersone ther	0	3	0
John Murray ther	0	3	0
Thomas Still in Denfield	0	3	0
Peter Chrisčie ther	0	3	0
John Mackie ther	0	3	0
John Mitchell ther	0	3	0
Andrew Wilsone ther	0	3	0
Alexander Mackie ther	0	3	0
Hector Ritchie in Clerkhill	0	2	0
	6	0	0

Grandhoms Family.

His walued rent being above £500, and under an £1000, is of poll	£12	6	0
Item, three sones, John, George, and James, their poll, with the generall poll,	5	8	0
Item, four danghters, Janet, Katherin, Margarat, and Anna, their poll is	1	4	0
Mr. James Smith, servant (no settled fee, no gentleman), of generall poll	0	6	0
Norman Nicoll, 32 merks per annum, fortieth part and generall poll	0	16	8
William Robertsone, 30 merks per annum, fortieth pairt whereof and generall poll	0	16	0

Elizabeth Falconer, 16 merks per annum, the fortieth pairt and generall poll ...	£0	11	4
Margarat Hector, the lyk fee and generall poll..	0	11	4
	£21	19	4

GEORGE BARTLET, younger in Grandhom, of valuatione 14s., with his oun and his wifes generall poll is..	£1	6	0
William Logie, servant, fee 22 merks, fortieth pairt and generall poll is.........	0	13	4
Alexander Craig, 10 merks per annum, fortieth part and generall poll is.........	0	9	4
Agnes Mackie, the lyk fee and poll	0	9	4
Andrew Chyne, subtennent, and his wife, their generall poll is....................	0	12	0
Margaret Jaffray, spouse to the said William Logie, her generall poll............	0	6	0
Peter Mackie, grassman, and his wife, their poll is.......................................	0	12	0
James Taylor, grassman and taylor, and his wife...	0	18	0
ALEXANDER WALKER, tennent at Mill of Grandhom, of valuatione is 3s., with his oun and his wifes generall poll..	0	15	0
William Nicoll, servant, £3 per annum, fortieth part and generall poll	0	7	6
Jean Ritchie, 10 merks per annum, fortieth part and generall poll is	0	9	4
	£6	17	10

DENSTOUNE.

Hector Ritchie, fermer, of valued rent 10s., with his oun and his wifes poll is...	£1	2	0
Alexander Allan, servant, £18 per annum, the fortieth part and generall poll ...	0	15	0
Robert Steven, £8 per annum, fortieth part and generall poll is.....................	0	10	0
Janet M'Intosh, £9 per annum, the fortieth part and generall poll is...............	0	10	6
Jean Watsone, subtennent (no stock, no servants, &c.), of generall poll	0	6	0
DAVID STILL, fermer, of vuluatione 10s., with his own and his own and his wyfes generall poll...	1	2	0
George Sympsone, servant, fee £8 per annum, fortieth part and generall poll is	0	10	0
Thomas Menzies and Jane Taylor, the like fee and poll	1	0	0
John Hector, subtennent (no trade nor stock), his generall poll	0	6	0
Jannet Christell, his spous (no children of age nor servants, &c.) generall poll...	0	6	0
Adam Jeans, subtennent (no trade or stock) and Elspeth Philp, his spous, poll	0	12	0
Jannet Yett, a widow woman, her poll is	0	6	0
	£7	5	6

PERSLIE.

Thomas Watt, fermer, of valued rent, with his own and his wifes generall poll...	£1	2	0
Item, two children, James and Thomas *in familia*, poll...............................	0	12	0
Elizabeth Mortoun, servant, £8 per annum, fortieth part and generall poll is ...	0	10	0
JAMES STILL, fermer, of valuatione 10s., with his own and his wyfes poll is...	1	2	0
George Still, his son *in familia*, of generall poll	0	6	0
Isobell Mortimer, servant, 14 merks per annum, fortieth pairt and generall poll,	0	10	8
JOHN FETTES, fermer in Perslie, of valued rent 10s., with his own and wifes poll,	1	2	0
George Mortimer, servant, £8 per annum, the fortieth pairt and generall poll...	0	10	0
William Thomsone, weaver, of valued rent 3s. (not layable for the samen, being higher classed) with his own and his wyfes generall poll is...............	0	18	0
	£6	12	8

8. PAROCH OF OLD MACHAR.

BRIGTOUN.

Alexander Watson, fermer (no trade or stock), of valued rent 8s., with his own and his sons generall poll, caled George, is	£1	0	0
John Christie, subtennent (no trade or free stock), with his own and wyfes generall poll	0	12	0
	£1	12	0

BUCKIE.

Andrew Sangster, fermer (no trade or free stock), of walued rent 8s., with the generall poll for himself and wife	£1	0	0
Item, two sons, William and Alexander (no servants, &c., their generall poll is	0	12	0
George Bartlet, elder, fermer, his free stock under 500 merks, of walued rent 8s., with his own and his wifes generall poll is	1	0	0
Item, his son James, his generall poll is	0	6	0
DAVID ANDERSONE (no trade or free stock), of valued rent 3s., with his own and his wifes generall poll	0	15	0
Elizabeth Gae, servant, fee £3 per annum, the fortieth part and generall poll is	0	7	0
JOHN MURRAY, fermer (no trade or stock), of walued rent 3s., with his own and his wifes generall poll	0	15	6
Thomas Hendrie, servant, £4 per annum, the fortieth part whereof and generall poll is	0	8	0
John Reid and Alexander Taylor, shoemakers, and their wives, generall poll is	1	16	0
John Oliphant (no trade or stock), and Christian Andersone, his spouse, poll is...	0	12	0
	£7	11	6

DENSFIELD.

Thomas Still, fermer, of valuatione 3s., with his own and his wifes generall poll,	£0	15	0
PATRICK CHRISTIE, fermer, of waluatione 3s., with his own and wifes poll	0	15	0
Thomas Robertsone, servant, £6 per annum, the fortieth pairt whereof and generall poll	0	9	0
Agnes Drum, servant, £6 per annum, the fortieth pairt and generall poll	0	9	0
John Mackie ther (no trade or stock), of valuatione 3s., with his oun and his wyfes generall poll	0	15	0
John Mitchell, at the Mill of Densfield, of waluatione 3s., with his oun and his wyfes generall poll	0	15	0
Gilbert Bisset, servant (no fee), his generall poll	0	6	0
Andrew Wilsone, of waluatione 3s., with his oun and his wyfes poll	0	15	0
Alexander Mackie, of waluatione 3s., with his oun and his wyfes poll	0	15	0
James Finnie, workman, and Elizabeth Chapman, his spouse, of generall poll,	0	12	0
William Robertsone (no trade nor stock), and Margarat Syme, his spouse, poll...	0	12	0
	£6	18	0

CLARKSHILL.

Hector Ritchie (no trade or free stock), of generall poll	£0	6	0
The hundred pairt of the valued rent is	0	2	0
Issobell Jamesone, his spouse, (no children, &c.), of generall poll	0	6	0
	£0	14	0

TOUN OF ABERDEEN FOR GILCOMSTOUNE.

The walued rent thereof is	£501	1	2

VIII. PRESBYTRIE OF ABERDEEN.

The hundred pairt whereof, payable in name of poll, is		£5	0	2
Proportionat amongst the tennents thus:—				
Imprimis, Jean Wachop, relict of Robert Menzies, at the Mill, her proportione of the valuatione is	£1	10	2	
William Catanach, in Meikle Gilcomstone	1	10	0	
William Bartlet, in Upper Gilcomstone	1	4	0	
John Blenshell, in Nether Gilcomstone	0	6	0	
Walter Forbes ther	0	6	0	
Donald Adam, in Loanhead	0	4	0	
		£5	0	2

Tennents and Subtennents of Gilcomstone.

Jean Wachop, at the Mill of Gilcomstone, whose husbands poll would have been £3, but she is not layable in payment of the third part therof, in regard she is higher classed, by paying the hundred part of the valued rent, which, with the generall poll, is	£1	16	2
Item, five children, William, Margarat, Jean, Mary, and Marjore, their generall poll is	1	10	0
Marjiore Brown, her mother, her generall poll is	0	6	0
James Findlay, servant, 40 merks per annum, the fortieth part and poll	0	19	4
James Sheepherd, 32 merks per annum, the fortieth part and generall poll	0	16	8
James Forbes, the like fee and generall poll	0	16	8
William Catto, £6 per annum, the fortieth part and generall poll	0	9	0
Jean Hutcheon, 14 merks per annum, the fortieth part and generall poll is	0	10	8
Elizabeth Mill, the like fee and generall poll	0	10	8
Elizabeth Wisheart, £8 per annum, the fortieth part with generall poll is	0	10	0
William Duguid, subtennent and millert, and his wife, poll is	0	18	0
William Catanach in Midle Gilcomstone, stock under 500 merks, of waluatione £1 10s., with his oun, and wife, and two children *in familia*, viz. Margarat and Elizabeth, their polls are	2	14	0
James Hay, servant, £20, fortieth part and generall poll	0	16	0
James Smith, £20, the fortieth part with the generall poll is	0	16	0
Peter Dounie, £16, the fortieth part with the generall poll is	0	14	0
William Watt, £6, the fortieth part with the generall poll is	0	9	0
Jean Tough, £8, the fortieth part and generall poll is	0	10	0
George Touch, subtennent and smith, and his wife, their poll is	0	18	0
WILLIAM BARTLET in Upper Gilcomstone (no trade or free stock), of valuatione £1 4s., his own, his wife, and George, his son *in familia*, poll is	2	2	0
William Thomsone, David Harrow, and Elizabeth Robertsone, servants, ilk ane £10 per annum, the fortieth part with the generall poll is	1	13	0
William Couper, subtennent (no free stock), for himself and his wife of poll is	0	12	0
George Skinner, subtennent (no free stock, &c.) for his own and his wifes poll	0	12	0
Alexander Chyne, subtennent (no free stock, &c.), his own and his wifes poll	0	12	0
William Russell, taylor (no free stock, &c.), his poll for his trade, with his oun and his wifes generall poll	0	18	0
James Munzie, shoemaker (no free stock), poll for his trade, with his oun and his wifes generall poll	0	18	0

10. PAROCH OF OLD MACHAR.

James Nicoll, subtennent (no trade, &c.), with his oun and his wifes poll	£0	12	0
Walter Forbes in Nether Gilcomstone (no trade nor stock), of waluatione 6s., with his oun and his wifes generall poll (no children of age)	0	18	0
John Blenshell ther (no trade or free stock), his generall poll is 6s., the hundred pairt of the valued rent is 6s., Elizabeth Crawfoord, his spouse, 6s., and an son called Thomas 6s. (no servants nor subtennents), in all is	1	4	0
Donald Adam in Loanhead (no trade, or free stock), his generall poll, with the hundred pairt of the valued rent being 4s., and Jean Chalmers, his spouse, her generall poll is	0	16	0
Robert Rae, servant, £20 per annum, the fortieth part and generall poll	0	16	0
Margaret Murray, 10 merks per annum, fortieth part and generall poll	0	9	4
Andrew Mitchell, Anna Forsyth, James Smith, Christian Fouler, pentioners	0	0	0
	£28	2	6

TOWN OF ABERDEEN, FOR RUTHRESTONE.

The valued rent for Ruthrestone is	£300	0	0
The hundreth pairt, payable be the tennents, is	£3	0	0
Andrew Bartlet, farmer (no trade, no stock), poll is	£0	6	0
The hundreth pairt of the valued rent, payable be him, is	3	0	0
Item, Margarat Robertsone, his spouse, poll	0	6	0
Andrew Godsman, servant, 25 merks per annum, fortieth part and generall poll,	0	7	6
James Fraser, £3 per annum, the fortieth pairt and generall poll is	0	14	4
Isobell Duncan, servant, for fee and generall poll	0	9	4
Janet Couper, £3 per annum, the fortieth part and generall poll is	0	7	6
William Webster, subtennent (no trade or free stock), his generall poll is	0	6	0
Margarat Spark, his spouse, her poll is	0	6	0
Euphemia Rogie, servant, £8 per annum, the fortieth pairt whereof and generall poll is	0	10	0
John Freeman, subtennent (no trade or free stock), his generall poll is	0	6	0
Marjiorie Troup, his spouse, her poll	0	6	0
Margarat Bain, servant, 10 merks, fortieth pairt and generall poll is	0	9	4
George Walker, subtennent (no trade or stock), poll is	0	6	0
Marjiorie Laing, his spouse, her poll is	0	6	0
John Hutcheon, subtennent (no trade or stock), poll	0	6	0
Jean Fyfe, his spouse (no children, no servant), her generall poll	0	6	0
James Farquharsone, shoemaker and subtennent, and Agnes Innes, his spouse, (no children, &c.) their poll, with the generall poll, is	0	18	0
John Davidsone, subtennent (no trade, &c.), and Jean Smith, his spouse, their generall poll is	0	12	0
	£10	8	0

Mr. Alexander Davidson for Berrihill and his fishing upon Don:—Berrihill and the fishing upon Don is of valued rent £400, whereof Berrihill is £68. The hundreth pairt whereof is ... £0 13 8

VIII. PRESBYTRIE OF ABERDEEN.

    Proportionat amongst the tennents thus:—
Imprimis, James Wisheart... £0 6 10
Alexander Gill... 0 6 10
                                                                                                 0 13 8

Tennents and Subtennents.

James Wisheart, fermer (no trade, no stock), his poll, with the hundred pairt of his valued rent, and Agnes Gill, his spouse, their poll is.................. £0 18 10
Three children, James, Thomas, and Isobell *in familia*, poll......................... 0 18 0
James Johnstone, servant, fee £12, fortieth part and generall poll.................. 0 12 0
John Laurenstone, with his wyfe (no children, &c.), and his oun generall poll... 0 18 0
ALEXANDER GILL, fermer (no trade nor stock), his generall poll and the hundred pairt of his walued rent, and Katherine Nicoll, his spouse, is.. 0 18 10
Peter Jackson, servant, fee £18, the fortieth pairt and generall poll............... 0 15 0
Alexander Robertson, fee £6, the fortieth pairt and generall poll.................... 0 9 0
Elizabeth Tillery, fee £8, the fortieth pairt and generall poll......................... 0 10 0
James Robertsone, subtennent (no trade), and Girsell Christell, his spouse, (no children, no servants, no stock, &c.) poll is.. 0 12 0
                                                                                £6 11 8

The walued rent for his Fishing upon Don is.. £332 0 0

The hundred pairt whereof is... £3 6 4
And payable be the said Maister Alexander Davidsone, as being in his oun hand, but he being classt in a higher capacity, is not layable, and living within the burgh of Aberdeen, is, with his family, pollable ther, or in the parioch of Culsamond, where the greatest pairt of his interest lyes.

JAMES GORDON of Seaton for his lands, the waluatione of lands being......... £266 13 4

The hundred pairt payable be the tennents, as followes, is........................... £2 13 4

    Imprimis, George Forsyth, elder, his proportione of his maisters waluatione is... £0 6 0
James Diverty... 0 6 0
William Harvie.. 0 2 0
Alexander Brow... 0 2 0
William Taylor.. 0 4 0
Thomas Taylor.. 0 3 0
Francis Irving... 0 6 0
William Chalmer.. 0 4 0
William Proctor... 0 4 0
Thomas Forsyth... 0 3 0
George Forsyth, younger... 0 4 0
John Smith.. 0 6 0

10. PAROCH OF OLD MACHAR.

John Still in Links	£0	2	0			
Alexander Troup ther	0	2	0			
				£2	14	0

James Gordon of Seaton his Family.

His valued rent being as said is £266 13s. 4d., his poll, with generall poll, is	£9	6	0
Marjorie Forbes, his lady, her poll is	0	6	0
Margaret Scougall, his grandchyld (no children *in familia*), her poll is	0	6	0
Robert Wisheart servant, fee £24, fortieth pairt and generall poll	0	18	0
William Murdo, £24 per annum, fortieth part and generall poll is	0	18	0
David Murray, 26 merks, per annum, fortieth part and generall poll is	0	14	8
Margarat Laurenston, 14 merks per annum	0	10	8
Elisabeth Charles, 7 merks per annum, fortieth part and generall poll	0	8	4
	£13	7	8

(James Gordon of Seatoun his half nets fishing upon Don, belonging now heretable to John Scougall, lymner in Edinburgh, but possest be the said James Gordon as tennent, is of valued rent £166 13s. 4d., the hundred pairt is £1 13s. 4d., but the said James Gordon is not layable, being polled in a higher capacity.)

Thomas Forsyth, wyver (no free stock), poll for his trade, his own and wife, a son called Thomas *in familia* (no servants, and is not layable for his waluatione, being classt in a higher capacity), is	£1	4	0
Andrew Forsyth (no trade), his wife and daughter *in familia*, poll	0	18	0
Francis Irving, flesher (stock under 500 merks), for his trade and his own and his wifes generall poll is	0	18	0
Alexander Finnie, servant, £16 per annum for fee, and generall poll (not layable for his proportione of the valued rent)	0	14	0
George Forsyth, elder, of waluatione 6s., with his own and his wifes poll is	0	18	0
Arthur Craighead, servant, £12 per annum, the fortieth part and generall poll,	0	12	0
Agnes Mill, his spous, poll is	0	6	0
Besse Crawfoord, 5 merks, for fee and generall poll	0	8	8
James Grhame, subtennent, his wife (no servants, &c.), their generall poll	0	12	0
George Brow, subtennent, and his wife, their poll is	0	12	0
Anna Brebner, relict of James Paull, of generall poll	0	6	0
Cloria Sangster, relict of Laury Chalmer, her poll	0	6	0
Item, two daughters *in familia*, their poll is	0	12	0
[ ], relict of [ ] Torry, workman, and her daughter *in familia*, poll is	0	12	0
JAMES DIVERTY, of waluatione 6s., with his own, his wife, and son *in familia*, called William, poll is	1	4	0
Isobell Rust, relict of William Johnstone, workman, her poll is	0	6	0
William Proctor ther, of valuatione 4s., with his own and his wifes generall poll,	0	16	0
William Harvie, of waluatione 2s., with his own and his wifes generall poll	0	14	0
Helen Andersone, relict of William Harvie, fisher, and daughter *in familia*, poll,	0	12	0
George Messone (no trade), Marjorie Messon, his spous, and Isobell Dyce, his daughter in law (no chyldreen of age, nor servants), for generall poll	0	18	0

VIII. PRESBYTRIE OF ABERDEEN.

George Forsyth, younger (no trade), with his oun and his wyfes generall poll, and his proportione of the waluatione, is	£0	16	0
George Gibb, taylor, and his wyfe (no chyld, &c.), their generall poll is	0	18	0
William Renie, shoomaker, and his wife, (no child, &c.), their generall poll is	0	18	0
Robert Walker, taylor, and his wyfe, their poll (no chyld)	0	18	0
Alexander Forsyth, weaver, and his wyfe, their poll is	0	18	0
Thomas Taylor (no trade or stock), and Isobell Ironsyd, his wife, and Jannet, his daughter *in familia*, their poll, with the hundred pairt of the valuatione, is	1	1	0
William Taylor, of waluatione 4s., with his oun and his wifes generall poll is	0	16	0
Alexander Brow, shoomaker (no stock, &c.) his waluatione is 9s., with his oun and his wifes generall poll, is	1	7	0
Peter Thomsone, flesher, and his spouse, their poll, having no childreen, &c.	0	18	0
James Anderson (no trade), and Marjiorie Troup, his spouse, generall poll is	0	12	0
John Bodie, shoomaker, and his wife (no chyld, &c.), of poll.	0	18	0
William Chalmer, flesher, Isobell Arbuthnott, his spouse, and two childreen, William and Isobell *in familia* (not layable to the waluatione), poll is	1	10	0
Christian Arbuthnot, relict of Alexander Forbes, merchant, her generall poll is	0	6	0
Mary Dun, servant, 7 merks per annum, fortieth part and generall poll is	0	8	4
William Inglis, wyver (no stock, no chyld, &c.), and Jannet Mowat, his spouse,	0	18	0
John Inglis, wyver, and Jannet Annand, his spouse, and [ ] Annand, his sister in law (no childreen, no servants, no stock), their generall poll is	1	4	0
William Craig, shoemaker, and his wife (no chyld, no servant, no stock), poll is	0	18	0
Alexander Arthur, messon, for his trade, his oun and his wifes generall poll, is	0	18	0
George Leslie, workman (no trade, &c.), and his spouse, ther generall poll	0	12	0
Robert Procter (no trade, &c.), and Barbara Watsone, his spouse, their poll is	0	12	0
Margarat Allan, relict of Alexander Robertson (no chyldreen, &c.) her poll is	0	6	0
Alexander Booth, shoomaker, and Jean Troup, his spouse (no chyld, &c.), poll,	0	18	0
John Crevie, merchant, (stock under 500 merks), and Jannet Allan, his spouse, and ane daughter *in familia*, poll	0	18	0
John Smith, blacksmith, and Jean Hogg, his spouse, their generall poll is	0	18	0
Two sons, John and Adam *in familia*, their poll is	0	12	0
John Mill, servant, £16 per annum, the fortieth part with generall poll	0	14	0
Thomas Tilliry, servant, £10 per annum, the fortieth pairt and generall poll	0	11	0
Margrat Gray, £8 per annum, the fortieth part and generall poll	0	10	0
George Walker, messon, and Christian Smith, his spouse, generall poll is	0	18	0
William Walker, prentice (no fee), his generall poll	0	6	0
Isobell Gray, servant, £4 per annum, the fortieth part and generall poll	0	8	0
Margarat Adam, £5 per annum, the fortieth pairt and generall poll is	0	8	6
	£38	2	6

(John Still and Alexander Troup are with their familyes, polled amongst the relict of Mr. William Moir his tennents.)

JAMES GORDON, brother to the Laird of Badenscoth, gentleman, his poll	£3	6	0
Margarat Moir, his spouse, and an daughter called Mary, poll is	0	12	0

10. PAROCH OF OLD MACHAR.

John Murray, servant, £4 per annum, the fortieth part and generall poll.........	£0	8	0
Elizabeth Milne and Jannet Petrie, ilk ane 16 merks per annum, the fortieth paint and generall poll is	1	2	8
	£5	8	8

EARLE OF PANMUIRE.

The waluatione of the said EARLE his Lands is £300	0	0	
The hundred pairt payable as poll is £3	0	0	

Proportioned among the tennents thus :—

Imprimis, Thomas Forbes of Tarbothill	£1	3	8	
John Chalmer in Upper Mendurno	1	8	4	
Agnes Innes, relict of Robert Smith, at the Mill of Mendurno ...	0	8	0	
				3 0 0

TARBOTHILL.

Thomas Forbes, fermer ther, and gentleman, whose free stock is under 5000 merks, poll with the generall poll is...	£3	6	0
Jean Summer, his spous, of generall poll	0	6	0
Item, five children in familia, Thomas, Alexander, Christian, Elizabeth, and Jean, their generall poll is	1	10	0
John Ferguson, servant, 26 merks the fortieth pairt whereof and generall poll is	0	14	8
John Hendrie, £10 per annum, the fortieth pairt whereof and generall poll is...	0	11	0
Bessie Brown, 20 merks per annum, the fortieth pairt and generall poll is	0	12	8
Isobell Davidsone, the like fee and poll is...	0	12	8
(The said Thomas is not layable in payment of his proportion of valued rent, being higher classed.)			
George Conan, subtennent, and his wife (no childreen of age), poll is	0	12	0
John Strogs, subtennent (no trade or free stock), Isobell Hendersone, his spous,	0	12	0
Thomas Gibson, subtennent (no trade or free stock), and Jean Hay, his spous...	0	12	0
Patrick Hendersone, subtennent and weaver, poll with the generall poll	0	12	0
Janet Gill, his spous (no child of age &c.), her generall poll is.....................	0	6	0
Alexander Hendersone, subtennent and weaver, and his wife, their poll is	0	18	0
James Morison, subtennent and taylor, his poll with the generall poll............	0	12	0
Margarat Massie, his spouse, and Thomas Morisone, his son, poll is...............	0	12	0
	£12	9	0

OVER MENDURNO.

John Chalmer, farmer, his free stock, under 500 merks of waluatione £1 8s. 4d., with his own and his wifes generall poll is	£2	0	4
Patrick Davidsone, servant, 14 merks, fortieth pairt and generall poll	0	10	8
John Barnet, £6, fortieth pairt and generall poll...	0	9	0
William Hervie, £4, fortieth pairt and generall poll	0	8	0
Isobell Webster (no children of age), fortieth pairt and generall poll is	0	10	0
George Caie, subtennent and weaver, his own and his wifes generall poll......	0	18	0
William Andersone, subtennent and shoemaker, his poll, with generall poll......	0	12	0
Jean Smith, his spouse (no children of age), her generall poll is	0	6	0
Thomas Tillery, subtennent (no trade or free stock), his generall poll is............	0	6	0
Jean Reid, his spouse (no children or servants in familia), poll is	0	6	0

VIII. PRESBYTRIE OF ABERDEEN.

Alexander Tait, subtennent (no trade or free stock, no children or servants,) with his own and his wife of generall poll	£0	12	0
Elizabeth Cristell, relict of Patrick Cristell, indweller in Balhelvie (no children, servants, &c.	0	6	0
Jean Jacksone, a widow (no stok, no children, &c.), poll is	0	6	0
Isobell Scott, relict of George Davidsone, millart at Mendurno (she has no children, servants, or stock)	0	6	0
William [ ], subtennent (no trade or free stock, no children, no servants), his own and his wifes generall poll is	0	12	0
Margarat Archie and Margarat Keith, pensioners	0	0	0
	£8	8	0

MILL OF MENDURNO.

Agnes Innes, relict of Robert Smith, her free stock under 500 merks, with the proportione of the valued rent, which is 8s., and generall poll is	£0	14	0
Thomas Mowat, servant, £12, fortieth pairt and generall poll is	0	12	0
Margaret Archie, £10, fortieth pairt and generall poll	0	11	0
Barbara Scott, £10, fortieth pairt and generall poll is	0	11	0
George Allan, subtennent (no trade, no free stock, no children of age, no servants), with his own and his wifes generall poll is	0	12	0
	£3	0	0

MASTER PATRICK SANDILANDS OF COTTON.

The said Mr. Patrick his lands being of valued rent	£293	6	8
The hundred pairt whereof payable in name of poll	£2	18	8

Proportionat amongst the possessours thus :—

Imprimis, Alexander Taylor in Cotton	£0	18	0
James Messon at Tilledron	0	10	0
Alexander Ferguson in Hillhead	0	6	0
James Marnoch in Old Aberdeen	0	4	0
Lucres Glennie ther	0	2	8
William Kilgour at the Walkmill	0	12	0
William Clerk at Gordons Mill	0	6	0
	2	18	8

Mr. Patrick Sandilands of Cotton, his Family.

His valued rent being as said is £293 6s. 8d., his poll, with the generall poll for himself, his lady, and eight childreen *in familia*, Patrick, William, George, Jean, Rachell, and Magdalen Sandilands, Marjorie Davidson, his daughter in law, and Gilbert Black, his grandchyld, is	£12	0	0
John Smith, his servant, fee £20, fortieth part and generall poll is	0	16	0
Thomas Massie and George Hird, the like fee and poll each	1	12	0
Jannet Benzie, 16 merks per annum, fortieth part and generall poll is	0	11	4
Agnes Davidsone and Mary Geddes, the like fee and poll each	1	2	8
	£16	2	0

COTTON.

Alexander Taylor, fermer (no trade or free stock), of waluatione 18s., with his oun and his wifes generall poll	£1	10	0

10. PAROCH OF OLD MACHAR.

Robert Skeen, his servant, fee £20, fortieth part and generall poll is...............	£0	16	0
Robert Bulfrit, servant, fee 14 merks, the fortieth pairt and generall poll is....	0	10	8
Agnes Dyce, servant, fee 10 merks, fortieth pairt and generall poll,................	0	9	4
James Reid, subtennent (no trade, stock, or children of age), his own and his wifes generall poll is..	0	12	0
Robert Pirie, subtennent, and his wife (no chyldreen of age), their poll is.........	0	12	0
Christian Blackall (not married, no stock, chyld, or servants,) poll is	0	6	0
Bessie Skeen and Jannet Broun, pentioners...	0	0	0
	£4	16	0

HILLHEID.

Alexander Fergusone, fermer, of waluatione 6s., with his oun and wifes generall poll (no children of age, &c.)...	£0	18	0

WAKMILL.

William Killgour, waxter (no trading stok), of waluatione 12s., with his oun and his wyfes generall poll..	£1	10	0
Two children, Peter and Jean *in familia*, their generall poll........................	0	12	0
George Hird, subtennent (no trade or stok), with his oun and his wifes poll......	0	12	0
	£2	14	0

GORDONS MILL.

William Clerk ther, millert (no stock), of waluatione 6s., with his oun and his wifes generall poll, is..	£1	4	0
James Andersone, prentice, his generall poll is...	0	6	0
Mary Piry, servant, fee £4, the fortieth pairt and generall poll.....................	0	8	0
	£1	18	0

(The forsaid James Messon, James Marnoch, and Lucres Glennie are polled in the toune of Old Aberdeen.)

LAIRD OF HILTON.

The said LAIRD of HILTONS walued rent in the parioch of Old Machar is....	£283	6	8
The hundred pairt thereof is..	£2	16	8

(And payable be the said Laird, conform to his obligatione thereanent.)

Hiltons Tennents in Ariburn.

William Bartlet, fermer (no trade, his stock under 500 merks), with his oun his wifes, and his sons, William, generall poll.................................	£0	18	0
William Robertson, servant, fee 10 merks, fortieth pairt and generall poll.......	0	9	4
Thomas Forsyth, £6 for fee, and poll..	0	9	0
Alexander Steven, 13 merks for fee, and poll................	0	10	4
James Robertsone, £4 for fee, and poll...	0	8	0
Christian Robertsone and Jean Wisheart, each £12 for fee, and poll..............	1	4	0
Alexander Andersone, weaver in Hilton, and Isobell Murray, his spouse, poll...	0	18	0
George Forsyth, subtennent (no trade, &c.), with his oun and his wifes poll...	0	12	0
John Ardes, subtennent, and his wife (no chyld of age, &c.), their generall poll,	0	12	0
Thomas Robertsone, subtennent, and his wife (no chyld, &c.), generall poll.......	0	12	0

VIII. PRESBYTRIE OF ABERDEEN.

Jannet Gibsone, relict of William Andersone, fermer in Newhills (no stock, chyld, &c.), her poll is	£0	6	0
Jean Mill (no stock, servant, &c.), her poll is	0	6	0
Christian Burges, pentioner	0	0	0
	£7	4	8

PERVINNES.

William Drum, fermer, and his wife and daughter (no trade, stock, &c.), poll is	£0	18	0
Alexander Wisheart, and his wife (no trade, stock, &c.), their generall poll	0	12	0
Peter Stott ther, and his wife and son, John (no trade, stock, &c.), poll is	0	18	0
John Hendrie ther, and his wife (no trade, stock, &c.), poll	0	12	0
John Young ther (no trade, no stock), his poll is	0	6	0
William Beverly, servant, of fee 5 merks, fortieth pairt and generall poll is	0	7	8
Isobell Mill, his mother *in familia*, her poll is	0	6	0
Andrew Nicoll ther, and his wife (no chyld of age, &c.), poll is	0	12	0
George Jameson, servant, fee £6, fortieth part whereof and generall poll is	0	9	0
Barbara Massie, servant, of fee £6, the fortieth pairt and generall poll is	0	9	0
William Duncan ther, and his wife (no children of age, &c.) their poll is	0	12	0
Thomas Still ther, and his wife (no chyldreen of age, &c.), their generall poll is	0	12	0
	£3	13	8

BODACHRAE.

John Greig, fermer ther, and his wife, their poll	£0	12	0
Item, an son Alexander *in familia* (no servants, &c.) his poll is	0	6	0
William Wilsone, subtennent (no trade or stock), and his wife, Bessie Robson,	0	12	0
Agnes Watson in Hilton, pentioner	0	0	0
Alexander Nicoll ther, and his wife (no trade, stock, &c.) their generall poll is	0	12	0
Item, three childreen *in familia*, viz. David, Jean, and Marjiorie, their poll is	0	18	0
Robert Smart ther, and his wife (no chyldreen of age, &c.), their generall poll is	0	12	0
James Yaitt ther, and his wife (no chyldreen of age, &c.), their generall poll is	0	12	0
William Murgan, and his wife (no chyldreen of age, &c.), their generall poll is	0	12	0
John Chyne ther, and his wife (no trade, stock, &c.), and daughter called Marjiore, their generall poll is	0	18	0
	£5	14	0

HILTON.

John Melvin, fermer (no trade or free stock), his oun and his wifes generall poll,	£0	12	0
Item, two chyldreen, John and Isobell, their generall poll is	0	12	0
James Gray, servant, £4 per annum, the fortieth pairt and generall poll	0	8	0
George Cushnie, fermer (no trade or stock), his poll	0	6	0
Barbra Logan, his spouse, polled in Old Aberdeen, in Mr. William Black's family (he has no chyld of age)	0	0	0
George Laing, servant, 4 merks per annum, the fortieth pairt and generall poll,	0	7	4
	£2	5	4

(The Laird of Hilton and his family polled in Newmachar.)

Mr. ANDREW MASSIE his fishing upon Don is of walued rent	£200	0	0
The hundred pairt thereof, payable in name of poll, is	£2	0	0

10. PAROCH OF OLD MACHAR.

And payable by himself (as being in his own hand), but he being polled in a higher capacity in the toun of Edinburgh, is not layable for this.

Relict of Mr. WILLIAM MOIR, for Links and the east syde of the Spittell, the valued rent of thes lands is.. £200 0 0

The hundred pairt thereof is... £2 0 0
Proportionat amongst the tennents thus :—
Imprimis, Alexander Troup, elder, in Links	£0	7	6
John Still ther...	0	8	6
John Seaton at the Keyston..	0	8	4
William Mitchell in Spittall East......................................	0	7	8
James Hill ther...	0	1	0
John Aiken at the Gallowgait Port.....................................	0	4	6
Agnas Mitchell in Old Aberdeen..	0	1	8
William Sangster ther..	0	1	0

2 0 0

Tennents in the Links.

Alexander Troup, elder (no trade or free stock), of waluatione 7s. 6d., with his own and his wifes generall poll is	£0	19	6
An sone, James *in familia*, his generall poll is..	0	6	0
Alexander Troup, younger, subtennent (no trade), his free stock under 500 merks, with his own and his wifes generall poll is...........................	0	12	0
Alexander Burn, servant, £16 per annum, the fortieth pairt and generall poll is	0	14	0
John Duncan, £4 in the yeir, being a beggar in the winter (no children of age, no women servants), the fortieth pairt with the generall poll is.........	0	8	0
John Still, fermer ther (no trade or free stock), of waluatione 8s. 6d., with his his own and his wifes generall poll is...	1	0	6
William Coban, servant, £16 per annum, the fortieth pairt and generall poll is	0	14	0
William Brown, £8 per annum, the fortieth part and generall poll is...............	0	10	0
Patrick Christie, 8 merks per annum, the fortieth pairt and generall poll is......	0	8	8
Elizabeth Gordon, 10 merks per annum, the fortieth pairt and generall poll is ...	0	9	4
Cloria Mackie, £4 per annum (no chyldreen), fortieth pairt and generall poll	0	8	0
George Robertsone, subtennent and weaver, with his own and his wyfes poll is	0	18	0

£7 8 0

KEYSTONE.

John Seatone, his free stock under 500 merks, of waluatione 8s. 4d. (no chyldreen of age), with his own and his wifes generall poll is.........................	£1	0	4
John Taylor, servant, £20 per annum, the fortieth pairt and generall poll.........	0	16	0
Alexander Hendrie, £8 per annum, the fortieth pairt generall poll	0	10	0
Jane Jamesone, £8 per annum, the fortieth pairt and generall poll is	0	10	0
Helen Catto, £8 per annum, the fortieth part and generall poll is..................	0	10	0
James Linton, subtennent (no trade or free stock, no chyldreen, &c.), with his own and his wifes generall poll is	0	12	0

£3 18 4

SPITTELL EAST.

William Mitchell (no trade or stock), of waluatione 7s. 6d., with his own and his wifes generall poll is......	£0	19	6
John Cow, servant, £8 per annum, the fortieth pairt and poll is......	0	10	0
Margarat Leslie, £8, (no children of age), fortieth pait and generall poll......	0	10	0
George Robertsone, elder, weaver (no free stock, no children of age, &c.) with his own and his wifes generall poll is......	0	18	0
John Robertsone, shoemaker, his free stock under 500 merks, with his own and his wifes generall poll is......	0	18	0
Margarat M'Koneiston, servant (no children of age), £8, the fortieth pairt and generall poll is......	0	10	0
Griger Forbes, shoemaker (no free stock, no children of age, &c.), his poll and generall poll for himself and wife is......	0	18	0
John Strachan, shoemaker (no free stock, no children of age, &c.), his poll, with the generall poll for himself and wife, is......	0	18	0
Andrew Haddon, weaver (no free stock), his poll, with the generall poll for himself and wife is......	0	18	0
A son, George Haddon, *in familia*, his poll is......	0	6	0
Robert Duncan, shoemaker (no free stock, no children of age, &c.), his poll, with the generall poll for himself and wife is......	0	18	0
John Dollas, shoemaker (no stock, no children of age, &c.), his poll, with the generall poll of himself and wife is......	0	18	0
Besse Robertsone, relict of David M'Conachie, weaver (no stock), poll for herself and two children *in familia*, viz. Peter and Margarat, is......	0	18	0
James Nairn, weaver (no stock, no children of age, &c.) his poll, with the generall poll for himself and wife is......	0	18	0
James Leslie, shoemaker (no stock, no children of age), with his own and his wifes generall poll is......	0	18	0
James Philp, shoemaker (no stock), with his own and his wifes generall poll is	0	18	0
Agnes Philp, servant, 8 merks, fortieth part and generall poll (no chyldreen)...	0	8	8
John Luckie, shoemaker (no stock), with his oun and his wifes generall poll, is	0	18	0
Agnes Fraser, servant, £8, the fortieth part and generall poll is......	0	10	0
Alexander Peter, shoemaker (no stock), with his own and his wifes poll, is......	0	18	0
Jean Peter, servant, £4, fortieth part and generall poll......	0	8	0
William Bruice, maltman (no stock), with his oun and his wifes generall poll,	0	18	0
Elizabeth Duncan, servant, £2 per annum, fortieth part and generall poll......	0	7	0
James Leslie, younger, shoemaker, his own and wifes poll (no chyldreen)......	0	18	0
Andrew Robertsone, wright (no stock), with his oun and his wifes generall poll,	0	18	0
James Touks, shoemaker (no free stock, chyldreen, or servants), with his own and his wifes generall poll, is......	0	18	0
James Hill, shoemaker (no stock), with his own and his wifes generall poll is...	0	18	0
Elspeth M'Grigor, servant, £4 per annum, fortieth part and generall poll......	0	8	0
(The hundreth pairt of his walued rent being 1s., he is not payable, in regaird he is polled in a higher capacity.)			
Robert Couts, gunsmith (no free stock), with his own and his wifes poll is......	0	18	0
Catherine Brebner, servant, £2, the fortieth part and generall poll......	0	7	0

10. PAROCH OF OLD MACHAR.

Isobell Craighead, relict of William Ritchie, her generall poll is.....................	£0	6	0
Gilbert Anderson, taylor (no free stock or chyldreen of age), with his own and his wifes generall poll, is..	0	18	0
Robert Thomsone, weaver (no free stok, or chyldreen of age), with his own and his wyfes generall poll, is..	0	18	0
William Aidie, shoomaker (no chyld, &c.), with his oun and his wifes poll......	0	18	0
James Robertson, workman (no chyld, &c.), with his oun and his wifes poll....	0	12	0
George Fyfe, shoomaker (no chyld, &c.), with his oun and his wifes poll.........	0	18	0
Alexander Moir, workman, and Elizabeth Maitland, his wife (no chyld, &c., is	0	12	0
Anthony Lowely, flesher (no free stock), his poll for himself and wife is..........	0	18	0
John Ligertwood, and his family; Christian Duncan, Christian Glennie; and Margarat Robertsone, and her family, all pentioners.......................	0	0	0
	£28	6	2

Master JOHN GORDON for his Fishing, his half-nets salmon fishing upon Don, is £166 13 4

The hundred pairt thereof is... £1 13 4
    Which is payable be himself (the said Fishing being in his oun hand), but, in regaird he is polled in a higher capacity in the Toun of Old Aberdeen, he is not layable for the payment of this.

RELICT of Mr. WILLIAM JOHNSTON for her Fishing, her half-nets salmon fishing upon Don, is.. £166 13 4

The hundred pairt thereof is... £1 13 4
    Which is payable be James Gordon of Seaton, as tacksman thereof, but he being polled in a higher capacity, is not layable for the payment of this. The said Relict of Mr. William Johnstone is now married to [   ] Irving of Beltie. They and their family are polled in the Shire of Mernes.

RELICT of Dr. MOIR, for Scotstoun; the walued rent of Scotstoun is............ £150 0 0

The hundred pairt thereof is... £1 10 0
    Proportionat amongst the tennents thus :—

Imprimis, Bessie Moir, in Scotston.......................................	£0	10	0
William Chalmer ther..	0	7	0
James Chalmer ther...	0	5	0
Alexander Chalmer ther...	0	2	6
Alexander Tilliry ther..	0	2	6
Edward Gill, in Cassie-end..	0	3	0
	1	10	0

Tennents and Subtennents of Scotstoun.

Bessie Moir, relict of Robert Chalmer, fermer ther, of waluatione 10s., with the generall poll for herself and two children, are...............................	£1	6	0
James Moir, servant, fee £8, the fortieth pairt and generall poll is.................	0	10	0

VIII. PRESBYTRIE OF ABERDEEN.

	£	s	d
Robert Gray, fee £4, the fortieth pairt and generall poll is	0	8	0
Jannet Gordon, fee £8, the fortieth pairt and generall poll is	0	10	0
William Brow, subtennent, and his wife (no trade, &c.), their generall poll	0	12	0
John Greig, subtennent, and his wife (no trade, &c.), their generall poll	0	12	0
William Chalmer, fermer (no trade, stock, &c.), of waluatione 7s., with his oun and his wifes generall poll, is	0	19	0
David Christall, servant, fee 22 merks, fortieth pairt and generall poll is	0	13	4
Margarat Brow, fee £8, the fortieth pairt and generall poll is	0	10	0
Elizabeth M'Pherson, fee 10 merks, the fortieth pairt and generall poll	0	9	4
James Chalmer, fermer ther (no trade or stock), with his oun and his wifes generall poll, and the hundred pairt of the walued rent, is	0	17	0
John Jeans, servant, fee 16 merks, the fortieth pairt and generall poll	0	11	4
William Andersone, fee £8, the fortieth pairt and generall poll	0	10	0
Marjiorie Leask and Bessie Brow, fee £8 each, fortieth pairt and generall poll,	1	0	0
Robert Still, subtennent (no trade or free stock), with his oun aud his wifes poll,	0	12	0
Alexander Chalmer, fermer (no trade or stock), of waluatione 2s. 6d., with his oun and his wifes generall poll	0	14	6
John Grig, serwant, £8 per annum, the fortieth part and generall poll is	0	10	0
William Mitchell, servant, £6 per annum, the fortieth part and generall poll,	0	9	0
Isobell Robertsone, 8 merks per annum, the fortieth pairt and generall poll is	0	8	8
George Grig, subtennent (no trade or stock, &c.), poll	0	6	0
Marjorie Walker, relict of William Mitchell, workman, and her daughter (no stock, no servants), their generall poll is	0	12	0
Alexander Tilliry, fermer, of waluatione 2s. 6d., with the generall poll for himself and wife is	0	14	6
Andrew Ritchie servant, £6 per annum, the fortieth pairt and generall poll is	0	9	0
Edward Gill in Cassie-end, of waluatione 3s., with the generall poll for himself and wife is	0	15	0
James Wilsone, servant, £4 per annum, the fortieth pairt and generall poll is	0	8	0
Alexander Massie, shoemaker, subtennent, and Katherine Gibson, his wife	0	18	0
William Gill, shoemaker, subtennent, and Barbara Laurenstone, his wife	0	18	0
Elizabeth Smith and Barbara Barnet, pentioners	0	0	0
	£17	4	8

Mr. GEORGE PEACOCK for Pitmuxton:—His Lands of Pitmuxton is of walued rent............ £120 0 0

The hundred pairt therof is............ £1 4 0
    Proportionat amongst the tennents thus:—

	£	s	d
Imprimis, William Walker ther	0	4	0
John Marr ther	0	3	0
Thomas Forbes ther	0	3	0
John Merser ther	0	2	0
George Davidsone ther	0	2	0
Alexander Brown ther	0	1	0
Patrick Youngsone ther	0	2	0

10. PAROCH OF OLD MACHAR.

Alexander Mackie in Hardgate	£0	2	0
James Davidsone ther	0	3	0
William Troup in Pitmuxton	0	2	0
	£1	4	0

Tennents and Subtennents of Pitmuxton.

William Walker, fermer (no trade or free stock), of waluatione 4s., with the generall poll for himself and wife, is	£0	16	0
Robert Craig, servant, £8 per annum, fortieth pairt and generall poll	0	10	0
William Keith, servant, 8 merks per annum, the fortieth pairt and generall poll	0	8	8
Peter Abernethie, subtennent (no trade or stock), with his oun and his wifes generall poll (no chyldreen of age, &c.)	0	12	0
Isobell Leonard, relict of William Youngsone, fisher, subtennent, her poll is	0	6	0
Jannet Geddes (no stock, childreen, or servants), poll	0	6	0
William Fraser, subtennent, with his own and his wifes generall poll	0	12	0
John Marr, shoomaker, of waluatione 3s., he not layable for the samen, being in a higher capacity, his generall poll for himself and wife, is	0	18	0
Alexander Craig, servant, of fee £6, the fortieth part and generall poll	0	9	0
Thomas Forbes, fermer, of waluatione, with the generall poll, is	1	7	0
John Merser, fermer (no trade or stock), of waluatione 2s., with the generall poll for himself, wife, and daughter Isobell, is	1	0	0
Christian Pitendrich, servant, £4 per annum, fortieth pairt and generall poll is	0	8	0
George Davidson, fermer, of waluatione 2s. (no chyldreen of age, servants, or subtennents), with his own, his wife, and Christian Mills his sister in law, generall poll, is	1	0	0
Alexander Broun, fermer, of waluatione 1s., with his own and his wifes generall poll (no chyldreen of age, no servants)	0	13	0
Patrick Youngsone, fermer (no trade or stock, no chyldreen of age, no servants), of waluatione 2s., with his own and his wifes generall poll	0	14	0
William Troup, fermer (no trade or stock), of waluatione 2s., with his own and his wifes, and two children, Alexander and Elisabeth, generall poll, is	1	6	0
(Alexander Mackie and his family are polled in New Aberdeen; James Davidson and his family are polled ther, as also Mr. Peacock, and his family.)			
	£11	5	8

JOHN LESLIE of Whytstryps his Lands of Whytstryps is of valued rent...... £110 0 0

The hundred pairt thereof is	£1	2	0

Proportionat amongst the tennents thus:—

Imprimis, James Drume of Whytstryps	£0	5	6
Alexander Hendrie ther	0	3	0
George Leslie ther	0	3	0
William Innes ther	0	3	0
George Still ther	0	3	0
James Still ther	0	3	0
James Nicoll ther	0	1	0
James Hendrie ther	0	0	6
	1	2	0

VIII. PRESBYTRIE OF ABERDEEN.

Tennents of *Whytstryps*

James Drum, farmer ther (no trade), stock under 500 merks, of valuatione 5s. 6d., with his own and wifes generall poll	£0	17	6
Item, two children, Richard and Margarat (no servants or subtennents), poll is	0	12	0
Alexander Hendrie, farmer, no trade, no stock, of valuatione 3s., with his own and his wifes generall poll	0	15	0
Agnes Mitchell, servant, £4 per annum, the fortieth pairt and generall poll is	0	8	0
George Leslie, farmer (no trade or free stock, no children of age, servants, &c.) of valuatione 3s., with his own and his wifes generall poll	0	15	0
William Innes, farmer ther (no trade or stock, no children of age, &c.) of waluatione 3s., with his own and his wifes generall poll	0	15	0
George Still, farmer (no trade or free stock), of waluatione 3s., with his own and his wifes generall poll is	0	15	0
Jean Watt, servant, 8 merks, fortieth pairt and generall poll	0	8	8
James Still, farmer ther (no trade or stock, no children of age, &c.) of waluatione 3s., with his own and his wifes generall poll is	0	15	0
James Nicoll, farmer (no trade or stock), of waluatione 1s., not having wife, children, &c., his poll is	0	7	0
James Hendrie, farmer ther (no trade or free stock, no children *in familia*, no servants, &c.) of waluatione 6d., with his own and his wifes generall poll	0	12	6
Janet Duncan, pentioner	0	0	0
	£7	0	8

ANDREW CASSIE, for his own and B. BLAKS Lands; the valuatione of the said Lands is	£58	0	0
The hundred pairt whereof is	£0	11	8

Proportionat amongst the Tennents, thus :—

Imprimis, Robert Din, in Seetone	£0	2	2
Isobell Cruickshank, in New Aberdeen	0	2	0
William Thomsone, in Old Aberdeen	0	2	0
Relict of David Nairn, in Old Aberdeen	0	2	6
James Thomsone, in Old Aberdeen	0	1	0
James Marnoch ther	0	2	0
	0	11	8

Andrew Cassies Family.

The said Andrew Cassies walued rent being £58, his oun and his wifes generall poll is	£4	12	0
Item, five children *in familia*, viz. Thomas, Duncan, Margarat, Elizabeth, and Jannet, their generall poll is	1	10	0
John Dugat, servant, £8 per annum, the fortieth part and generall poll	0	10	0
Edward Watsone, subtennent (no stock, trade, &c.), with his wife and his oun generall poll (no childreen of age, &c.)	0	12	0
Robert Din is out of the country, *animo remanendi*	0	0	0
	£7	4	0

10. PAROCH OF OLD MACHAR.

Master WILLIAM ROBERTSON, for Peterston :—His Lands of Peterstoun is of walued rent £50 0 0

The hundred pairt therof is... £0 10 0
And payable by George Aberdeen, tennent, who with his family do live in Old Aberdeen, and are polled ther; the said Mr. William is dead, and hes no representatives.

Aires of JOHN MOIR of Barnnes for Sunisyde :—The Lands of Sunisyde is of walued rent £45 0 0

The hundred pairt thereof is... £0 9 0
Proportionat amongst the tennents thus :—
Imprimis, Andrew Aberdeen in Sunisyde............................... £0 5 6
Robert Chalmer in Stankyaird 0 3 6
                                   0 9 0

Tennents of Sunisyde.

Andrew Aberdeen, fermer (no trade, stock under 500 merks), of walued rent 5s. 6d., with the generall poll for himself and wife, is £0 17 6
Alexander Guthrie, servant, £17 per annum, fortieth pairt and generall poll ... 0 14 6
John Summer, 20 merks per annum, the fortieth pairt and generall poll is...... 0 12 8
Jannet Brow, £4 per annum, the fortieth pairt and generall poll 0 8 0
Robert Chalmer in Stankyaird, fermer (no trade), of waluatione 3s. 6d., with his oun and wifes generall poll is... 0 15 6
William Black, servant, £20 per annum, fortieth pairt and generall poll is... 0 16 0
Anna Black, £10 per annum, the fortieth pairt and generall poll is 0 11 0
John Gibb, shoemaker (no stock), with his own and his wifes generall poll...... 0 18 0
                                  £5 13 2

WEST SYDE OF THE SPITTEL.

James Baverly, meason (no stock, &c.) with his own and wifes generall poll ... £0 18 0
John Mill (no trade, no stock), with his own and wifes generall poll 0 12 0
Item, Elspet Beverly, daughter to the forsaid James Baverly is 0 6 0
Alexander Simpsone, taylor (no stock), with his own, wife, and daughter *in familia*, their generall poll is... 1 4 0
James Hay, weaver (no stock), with his own and his wifes generall poll is 0 18 0
James Johnstone, shoemaker, with the poll for himself, wife, and daughter...... 1 4 0
William Findlater, shoemaker (no free stock), with the generall poll for himself and wife, and an son, William, is 1 4 0
Alexander Pyet (no trade or stock), with his own and his wifes generall poll ... 0 12 0
William Bennet, shoemaker (no free stock), with his own and his wifes poll 0 18 0
Elizabeth Ritchie, relict of George Fuller, shoemaker, her poll is 0 6 0
James Aberdour, smith, with his wife (no child, &c.), poll 0 18 0
Archibald Raff, gunsmith, with the generall poll for himself and wife is 0 18 0
William Sheepherd, shoemaker (no free stock), his poll for himself and wife is 0 18 0
Isobell Watsone, servant, 8 merks per annum, fortieth pairt and generall poll... 0 8 8
                                  £11 4 8

FROSTERHILL.

Andrew Hall, flesher (no free stock), his generall poll	£0	12	0
Item, his wife and an daughter, Agnes *in familia*, poll is	0	12	0
Willam Mackie, servant, 10 merks per annum, and generall poll	0	9	4
Alexander Dey, workman (no trade or free stock), with his oun and his wifes generall poll (no chyldren, &c.), is	0	12	0
Jonn Innes, blacksmith (no free stock, &c.), with his oun and his wifes poll	0	18	0
John Clerk (no trade, free stock, or chyld, &c.), with his oun and his wifes poll,	0	12	0
Andrew Keith, shoomaker (no free stock), with his oun and his wifes poll	0	18	0
Two children *in familia*, Elizabeth and Jean, their generall poll is	0	12	0
Gilbert Clerk, fermer (no trade, no free stock), with his oun, his wife, and daughter, Jean, *in familia* (no servants), their poll is	0	18	0
Alexander Munzie, fermer (no trade nor free stock), with his oun, his wife, and daughter, Agnas, their poll is	0	18	0
Alexander Hendrie, fermer, and Marjiorie Main, his spouse (no trade, &c.), poll,	0	12	0
William Thomsone, fermer (no trade, &c.), with his oun and his wifes poll	0	12	0
Robert Boddell, workman (no trade, &c.), with his oun and his wifes poll	0	12	0
John Skeen (no trade or free stock), with his oun, his wifes, and son, James, *in familia*, their generall poll is	0	18	0
David Webster (no trade or stock), and James and Alexander, his sons, *in familia*, their generall poll	0	18	0
Jannet Webster, servant, fee £8, the fortieth pairt and generall poll	0	10	0
James Couts (no trade, no stock, &c.), with his oun and his wifes generall poll,	0	12	0
John Downie, and his family, pentioners	0	0	0
	£11	15	4

JUSTICE MILLS.

James Davidson, fermer (no trade or free stock), with his oun and his wifes poll,	£0	12	0
Alexander Bannerman, servant, 20 merks, fortieth part and generall poll is	0	12	8
Isobell Leaper, £8 per annum, fortieth part and generall poll is	0	10	0
Marjorie Fothringhame, relict of Patrick Davidsone, fermer (no chyldreen of age, no free stock, no subtennents), her poll is	0	6	0
John Fothringame, servant, for fee and generall poll is	0	12	8
James Mill, 20 merks, fortieth part and generall poll	0	12	8
Margarat Dunbarr, £8, fortieth part and generall poll	0	10	0
	£3	16	0

CABERSTON.

Peter Aberdeen, fermer (no trade, no chyldreen of age, no subtennents), with his own and his wyfes generall poll	£0	12	0
Alexander Lyes, servant, £8, fortieth part and generall poll	0	10	0
Andrew Still, £4, fortieth part and generall poll is	0	8	0
Isobell Davidson £8, for poll is	0	10	0
	£2	0	0
Summa of OLD MACHAR Paroch is	£431	3	0

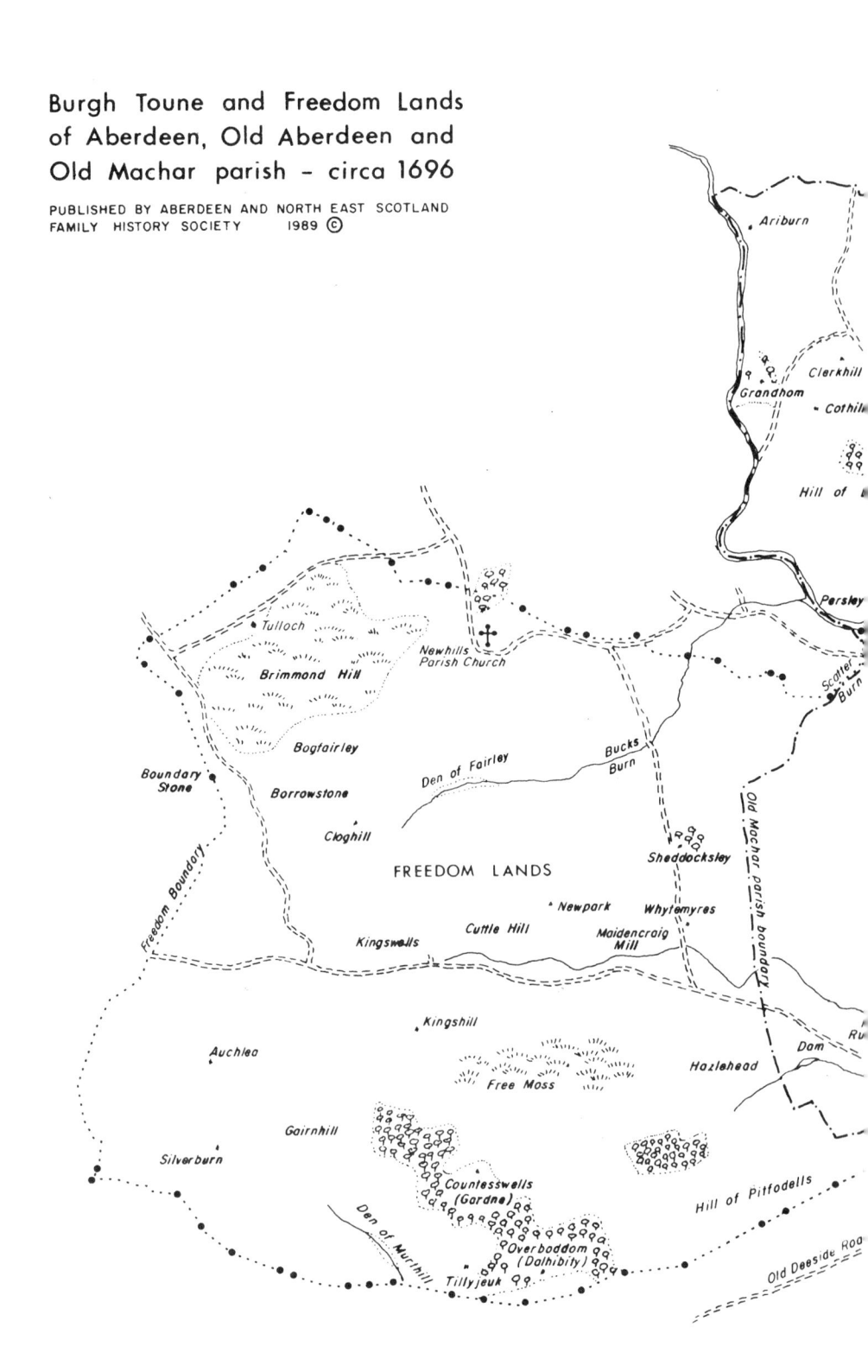

Burgh Toune and Freedom Lands of Aberdeen, Old Aberdeen and Old Machar parish – circa 1696

PUBLISHED BY ABERDEEN AND NORTH EAST SCOTLAND FAMILY HISTORY SOCIETY 1989 ©

Ariburn

Clerkhill
Grandhom
Cothil
Hill of
Persley
Tulloch
Newhills Parish Church
Brimmond Hill
Scatter Burn
Bogfairley
Bucks Burn
Boundary Stone
Borrowstone
Den of Fairley
Cloghill
Sheddocksley
FREEDOM LANDS
Newpark   Whytemyres
Kingswells   Cuttle Hill   Maidencraig Mill
Freedom Boundary
Old Machar parish boundary
Kingshill
Auchlea
Dam
Free Moss
Hazlehead
Ru
Gairnhill
Silverburn
Countesswells (Gardne)
Hill of Pitfodells
Den of Murthill
Overboddom (Dalhibity)
Tillyjeuk
Old Deeside Road

LOCATION MAP

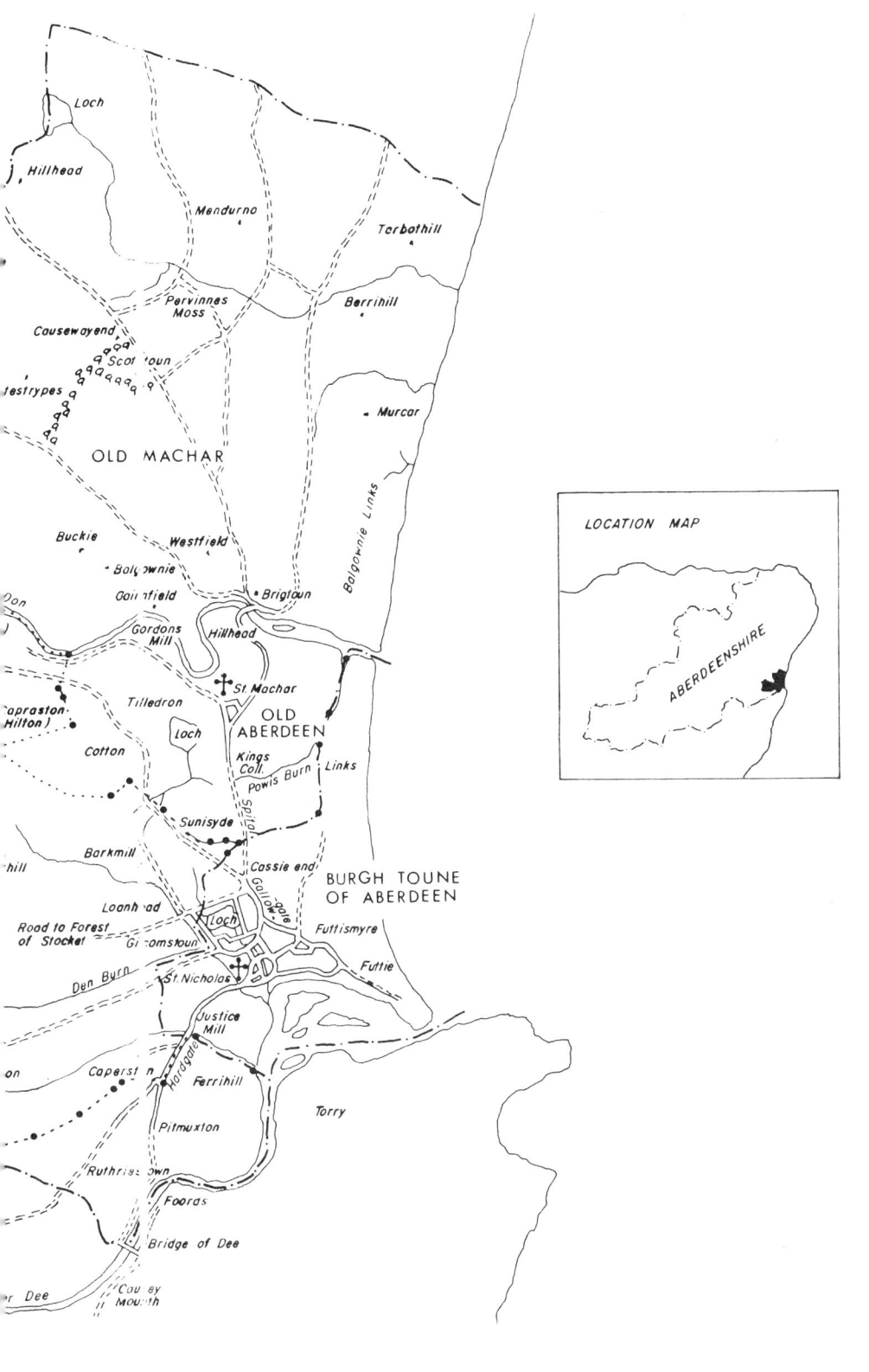

ABERDEENSHIRE

Loch
Hillhead
Mendurno
Tarbothill
Pervinnes Moss
Berrihill
Causewayend
Scotstoun
estrypes
Murcar
OLD MACHAR
Balgownie Links
Buckie
Westfield
Bolgownie
Don
Gainfield
Brigtoun
Gordons Mill
Hillhead
apraston (Hilton)
Tilledron
St. Machar
OLD ABERDEEN
Loch
Cotton
Kings Coll.
Powis Burn
Links
Sunisyde
Spital
Barkmill
hill
Cassie end
BURGH TOUNE OF ABERDEEN
Loanhead
Loch
Gallowgate
Road to Forest of Stocket
Gilcomstoun
Futtismyre
Den Burn
St. Nicholas
Futtie
Justice Mill
Hardgate
Caperston
Ferrihill
on
Pitmuxton
Torry
Ruthrieston
Foords
Bridge of Dee
Dee
Cousey Mouth

STATISTICS

MALES	758
FEMALES	931
UNSPECIFIED	98
TOTAL	1787

AN LIST of the POLABLE PERSONS within the TOUNE of OLD ABERDEEN, given up be Mr. ALEXANDER FRASER and JAMES KNIGHT, Bailies in Old Aberdeen, two Commissioners nominat and appointed for that effect, and be Mr. JOHN ROBERTSONE, Bibliothicarian of the said Toune, Clerk and Collector appointed be them for the said Toune.

IMPRIMIS, James Hervie, weaver ther, and his wife	£0	18	0
Alexander Hill, shoemaker ther, and his wife, poll	0	18	0
Sara Cuming, his servant, for fee and generall poll	0	10	0
James Turriffe, taylor ther, and his wife, poll	0	18	0
Alexander Strachan and Alexander Christie, indwellers ther, and their wives, poll is	1	4	0
Thomas Thomson, glover in Colledge Bounds, and his wife and daughter, poll	1	4	0
Elspet Patersone, servant, for fee and generall poll	0	8	0
Agnes Beverly, relict of Alexander Hatt, farmer in Old Aberdeen, and William and George Hats, her sons	0	18	0
Alexander Yeatt, her servant, for fee and generall poll	0	14	0
Cloria Bullfoord, her servant, for fee and generall poll	0	9	0

VIII. PRESBYTRIE OF ABERDEEN.

George Mill, indweller ther, and his wife, and son, John Mill *in familia*, and John Daniell, their servant, whose fee is £10, poll in all	£1	9	0
William Cruickshank, wheelwright, and his wife	0	18	0
George Barber, smith ther, and his wife, poll	0	18	0
Christian More, his servant, for fee and generall poll	0	7	4
Robert Sinclar and James M'Castell, taylors ther, and their wives, poll	1	16	0
William Gray, wheelwright ther, and his wife and daughter, poll is	1	4	0
Andrew Gray, younger, couper, and his wife, poll	0	18	0
George Cuming, smith, and his wife, poll	0	18	0
James Nicoll, wright ther, and his wife, and Agnes Watt, his servant, whose fee is £10 per annum, their poll	1	7	4
John Marnoch, litster ther, and his wife, poll	0	18	0
James Laing, indweller ther, and his wife, poll	0	12	0
John Sangster, bookbinder, and his wife, poll	0	18	0
John Leask, younger, weaver ther, and his wife, and William and John Leasks, his sons, poll is	1	10	0
John Ritchie, wright ther, and his wife, poll	0	18	0
John King, indweller ther, and his wife, and son Patrick King, their poll	0	18	0
William Anderson, flesher ther, and his wife and son, and Isobell Grant, servant, whose fee is £8 per annum, poll	1	14	0
James Mathewson ther, and his wife, poll	0	12	0
Thomas Smith, indweller ther, and his wife, poll	0	12	0
John Elles, weaver ther, and his wife	0	18	0
Robert Elphinstone, shoomaker in Colledge Bounds, and his wyfe, poll is	0	18	0
Margrat Marischall, relict of John Christell, indweller ther, her poll	0	6	0
Jean Chalmer, relict of Patrick Cheyne, indweller in Old Aberdeen, poll for herself, and two daughters *in familia*, is	0	18	0
Alexander Bruice, her servant, for fee and generall poll	0	8	0
Elizabeth Catto, servant, for fee and generall poll	0	10	0
Anna Robertson, relict of George Lovie, taylor ther, and her daughter, Margaret Lovie, poll	0	12	0
James Moor, weaver in College Bounds, and his wyfe	0	18	0
John Smith, shoemaker ther, and his wife	0	18	0
James Mill, maltman ther, and his wife, poll	0	18	0
Bessie Thomsone, his servant, for fee and generall poll	0	10	8
Marjorie Hill, relict of John Couper, bailie in Old Aberdeen, her house and free stock above 500 merks, but not extending to 5000 merks, poll is	1	2	8
Item, three children, Alexander, Margrat, and Agnes Coupers	0	18	0
Janet Fiffe, her servant, for fee and generall poll	0	8	0
George Breck, taylor, and his wife, poll	0	18	0
Thomas Adam, shoomaker, and his wife, poll	0	18	0
John Lawrensone, merchant ther (no stock), and his wife	0	12	0
Andrew Dyce, merchant ther, his free stock being above 500 merks, but not extending to 5000 merks, his poll, with the generall poll for his wife, is	3	2	0
Three children *in familia*, their poll	0	18	0
Anna Logie, servant, for fee and generall poll	0	10	0

12. TOUNE OF OLD ABERDEEN.

James Johnstone, merchant ther, his free stock being above 500 merks, but not extending to 5000 merks, poll for himself and wife, is	£3	2	0
Item, an sone, and Helen Dour, servant, whose fee is £8 per annum, *inde* for fee and generall poll	0	16	0
John Slidders, indweller ther, and his wife, poll	0	12	0
Margrat Gibsone, his servant, for fee and generall poll	0	10	8
Andrew Adam, shoemaker ther, and his wife, poll	0	18	0
Robert Lowe, merchant there, whose free stock is above 500, but not above 5000 merks, poll for himself, his wife, and three children *in familia*	4	0	0
Item, tuo servants, Christian Simer and Elspet Webster, fee £8 each, poll	1	0	0
James Robertsone, merchant ther, and his wife, poll	0	12	0
Margrat Ingliss and Marjiorie Forsyth, servants, for fee and generall poll	1	0	0
James Measson, maltman ther, and his wife, poll	0	18	0
Patrick Fife, his servant, for fee and generall poll is	0	14	0
Jean Wilsone and Agnes Rogie, servants, for fee and generall poll is	1	2	8
David Murray, measson ther, and his wife	0	18	0
Item, Janet Simpsone, servant, for fee and generall poll	0	10	0
Jean Hunter and Jean Walker, servants, for fee and generall poll is	1	0	0
John Elmsly, weaver in Colledge Bounds, and his wife, poll	0	18	0
James Fraser and William Ritchie, weavers in Old Abedeen, and their wives, poll is	0	18	0
Agnes Chalmer, indweller ther, and her daughter	0	12	0
Thomas Buchan, weaver in Colledge Bounds, and his wife, poll	0	18	0
Jean Carngill, servant, for fee and generall poll	0	10	0
George Robertsone, shoemaker, and his wife	0	18	0
George Massie, coppersmith, and his wife, poll	0	18	0
James Dickie, taylor ther, and his wife	0	18	0
Christian Thomsone, his servant, for fee and generall poll	0	10	0
Helen Cattanach, relict of George Leith, couper in Old Aberdeen, her poll	0	6	0
Margrat Knoues, relict of William Anderson, weaver ther, and Agnes Andersone, her daughter	0	12	0
John Lovie, taylor, and his wife, poll	0	18	0
Marjiorie Taylor, for fee and generall poll is	0	8	0
William Smith, younger, blacksmith, and his wife	0	18	0
Robert Collace, indweller ther, and his wife, and Katheren and Isobell Collace, his daughters, poll	1	4	0
Andrew Craigheade, merchant ther, and his wife	0	12	0
James Mill, flesher ther, and his wife, poll	0	18	0
Marjiorie Couper, relict of William Watt, caper ther, her poll is	0	6	0
John Ferguson, flesher in College Bounds, and his wife, and son Alexander, poll	1	4	0
Jean Sangster, his servant, for fee and generall poll	0	10	8
Alexander Anderson, weaver in Old Aberdeen, and his wife	0	18	0
George Garioch, taylor ther, and his wife, poll	0	18	0
George Ronald, merchant ther, and his wife (no free stock)	0	12	0
Item, Jean Ronald, his daughter, poll	0	6	0
Janet Gordon, his servant, for fee and generall poll	0	9	4

4 E

VIII. PRESBYTRIE OF ABERDEEN.

Robert Drum, indweller ther, and his wife, poll	£0	12	0
William Robertson, indweller ther, and his wife and sone, poll	0	18	0
James Jaffray, gardener ther, and his wife, poll	0	18	0
Alexander Jaffray, his brother *in familia*, poll	0	6	0
Item, ane servant, fee £2 per annum, the fortieth pairt with the generall poll is	0	7	0
Marjorie Simer, for fee and generall poll	0	10	8
Item, [ ] Cuming, for fee and generall poll is	0	7	0
Elspet Johns, relict of John Jaffrey, in Old Aberdeen, her poll is	0	6	0
Margrat Johns, servant, for fee and generall poll	0	9	0
John Wisheart, merchant ther, and his wife, poll	0	12	0
William Wilsone, maltman, and Alexander Christell, wright, and their wives	1	16	0
James Black, indweller ther, and his wife	0	12	0
Katheren Gordon, relict of Mr. James Gordon, merchant at Rothemay, whose poll (if alive) would have been £9, the third pairt wherof payable by the said Kathren is, with the generall poll	3	6	0
Item, Lues Gordon, her son, ane gentleman, poll	3	6	0
Item, George Gordon, his brother, poll	0	6	0
Isobell Bartlet, her servant, for fee and generall poll	0	7	6
George Cruickshank, thesaurer, his free stock above 500 but not 5000 merks, and Barbra Finnie, his spouse, poll	3	2	0
Item, three childreen *in familia*, poll	0	18	0
Item, Janet Aldman and Elspet Andersone, servants, for fee and generall poll,	1	2	0
John Dey, indweller in Colledge Bounds, and his wife	0	12	0
Item, Barbra Steinsone and Elizabeth Cheyne, servants, for fee and poll	1	0	0
John Walker, weaver ther, and his wife, and Jean Walker, his daughter, poll,	1	4	0
Donald Ross, weaver in Old Aberdeen, and his wife	0	18	0
David Gruer, merchant ther, whose free stock is above 500 merks, but does not extend to 5000 merks, for himself and wife	3	2	0
Item, five children *in familia*, poll	1	10	0
Elizabeth Allan, his servant, for fee and generall poll	0	10	0
George Taylor, indweller ther, and his wife, poll	0	12	0
John Watson, taylor, and his wife, poll	0	18	0
Alexander Watsone and William Murray, servants, for fee and generall poll	0	16	0
William Crombie and Peter Falconer, indwellers ther, and their wives, poll	1	4	0
Robert Forbes of Glencarvie, gentleman ther, and his wife, their poll is	3	12	0
Andrew Jameson, taylor ther, and his wife	0	18	0
George Killgoure, church beddall ther, he being a pentioner in the said church, and Bessie Innes, his spouse, the said George being a nottar, his poll, and generall poll, and wyfes, is	4	12	0
Item, Christian and Jean Murisons, each of their fees 16 merks per annum, poll is	1	2	8
Janet Smith, relict of Thomas Mitchell, indweller ther, her poll is	0	6	0
Bessie Andersone, her servant, for fee and generall poll	0	10	0
Helen Davidsone, relict of James Gibsone, weaver ther	0	6	0
Margrat Cuie, relict of William Angus, weaver ther, and Janet Angus, her daughter, poll	0	12	0

12. TOUNE OF OLD ABERDEEN.

Robert Shand, indweller ther, and his wife, poll	£0	12	0
William Innes and Thomas Shirres, weavers, and their wives, poll	1	16	0
Andrew Charles, weaver ther, and his wife	0	18	0
[ ], a servant, 10 merks per annum	0	9	4
Alexander Hervie, weaver ther, and his wife, poll	0	18	0
John Bisset, shoomaker, and his wife, and Margrat Bisset, his daughter, poll is	1	4	0
Janet Ross, his servant, for fee and generall poll	0	8	0
Lucres Glennie, relict of William Marnoch, indweller ther, her poll is	0	6	0
Margrat Sinier, her servant, for fee and generall poll	0	9	4
Alexander Mathewsone, indweller ther, and his wife, poll	0	12	0
Mr. William Cuming, master of the Musicle School, his poll, as being ane gentleman, is	3	6	0
John Kinard ther, and his wife, poll is	0	18	0
Marjiorie Irving, relict of John Fraser ther, he being a gentleman, her poll is	1	6	0
William Nicoll, indweller ther, and his wife	0	12	0
Elspet Stewart, relict of John Stewart, indweller ther, her poll is	0	6	0
George Allan, shoomaker ther, and his wife, poll	0	18	0
William Moir, indweller ther, and his wife, poll	0	12	0
William Cruickshank, flesher ther, and his wife	0	18	0
Robert Forbes, servant, for fee and generall poll is	0	7	0
Andrew Massie, merchant ther, and his wife, poll	0	12	0
John Leslie, belt weaver, and his wife, poll	0	18	0
William Thomsone, merchant ther, and his wife (no free stock)	0	12	0
Marie Elmsly, his servant, for fee and generall poll	0	10	0
Margrat Low, for fee and generall poll is	0	10	0
John Cowper, maltman in Old Aberdeen, poll is	0	12	0
Agnes Deins, relict of David Nairne, indweller ther, her poll is	0	6	0
Alexander Glass, indweller ther, and his wife, poll is	0	12	0
John Johnstone, taylor ther, poll	0	12	0
Robert Cooke, taylor ther, and his wife, poll	0	18	0
John Ross, merchant ther, and his wife, poll	0	12	0
William Elles, weaver in College Bounds, and his wife	0	18	0
Doctor James Garden, professor of Divinity in the Kings Colledge of Aberdeen, gentleman, and his lady, and nine children, poll	6	6	0
Jean Gordon, servant, for fee and generall poll	0	11	4
Margrat Mill, servant, for fee and generall poll	0	9	4
Anna Mitchell, relict of George Hunter, merchant in Old Aberdeen, whose poll (if alive) would have been £2 10s., and the said Anna being layable for the third part thereof, poll is	1	2	8
Margarat Hunter, her daughter, heiress to her father, her poll is	2	16	0
James Duguid, wright ther, and his wife, poll is	0	18	0
Elizabeth Sinclar, his servant, for fee and generall poll	0	9	0
George Aberdeen, indweller ther, and his wife, poll	0	12	0
Thomas Swaps, his servant, for generall poll	0	15	0
Margaret Mill, his servant, for fee and generall poll	0	9	4
Margrat Davidson, relict of William Anderson, weaver, her poll is	0	6	0

VIII. PRESBYTRIE OF ABERDEEN.

Elspet Thom, indweller ther, her poll is...	£0	6	0
Robert Ross, saddler ther, and his wife, poll is..	0	18	0
Isobell Muskie, his servant, for fee and generall poll.................................	0	10	0
Alexander Lundie, litster, his wife, and Mariorie Lundie, his daughter, poll is	1	4	0
Katherine Thomson, servant, for fee and generall poll...............................	0	8	8
Helen Thome, indweller ther, her generall poll...	0	6	0
Isobell Mathewson, relict of William Gray in Cottone, her poll is..................	0	6	0
Andrew Baxter, indweller ther, and his wife, poll.....................................	0	12	0
Isobell Patersone, for fee and generall poll..	0	9	0
Alexander Lintone, wright ther, and his wife and sone, their poll................	1	4	0
James Litlejohn, indweller ther, and his wife, poll...................................	0	12	0
Margrat Gordon, relict of Mr. John Lundie, humanist in the Kings Colledge of Aberdeen, whose poll would have been £3, the third pairt whereof payable by her..	1	6	0
Elspet Cumming, relict of James Christie, merchant ther, her poll for herself and daughter is...	0	12	0
James Ironsyde and Elspet [ ], her servants, for fee and generall poll......	1	0	0
Thomas Umphra, shoemaker ther, and his wife..	0	18	0
Alexander Midleton ther, and his wife, poll	0	18	0
Elisabeth Cruickshank, relict of William Gordon, indweller ther, her poll is...	0	6	0
Katheren Mitchell, relict of John Darge, poll	0	6	0
Isobell Lawson, relict of Robert Wilsone ther..	0	6	0
Isobell and Margrat Skeens, indwellers ther, poll......................................	0	12	0
James Marnoch, maltman ther, and his wife, poll.....................................	0	18	0
Alexander Murisone, his servant, for fee and generall poll..........................	0	15	4
William Smith, his servant, for fee and generall poll.................................	0	12	8
Christian Smith, his servant, for fee and generall poll...............................	0	10	8
Christian Still, relict of William Mackie, janitor of the Kings Colledge, poll is	0	6	0
Jean Deans, her servant, for fee and generall poll.....................................	0	10	0
Elspet Still, her servant, for fee and generall poll.....................................	0	9	0
William Jeans, merchant ther (no free stock), and Isobell Mitchell, his spouse, poll	0	12	0
George Mitchell, his brother-in-law, his poll	0	6	0
Christian Forsyth, servant, for fee and generall poll	0	10	0
George Laing, indweller ther, and his wife, poll	0	12	0
David Nicol, his servant, for fee and generall poll	0	15	0
Margrat Hill, his servant, for fee and generall poll	0	10	0
John Gray, baxter ther, his poll is	0	12	0
Margrat Lesly, relict of James Cullen, shoemaker ther, her poll is	0	6	0
Gilbert Broune, indweller ther, and his wife...	0	12	0
George Thome, messone ther, and his wife, poll	0	18	0
Margrat Beaverly, relict of Andrew Elmsly, in Old Aberdeen, her poll is......	0	6	0
James Diverty, her servant, for fee and generall poll	0	12	0
Marjiorie Forsyth, her servaut, for fee and generall poll	0	9	0
William Beverley, shoemaker ther (dead), and his wife, poll	0	18	0
Item, William Montgomrie, measson, and his wife, poll	0	18	0

12. TOUNE OF OLD ABERDEEN.

Duncan Cassie, indweller ther, and his wife, poll..	£0	12	0
Marjiorie Inglish, his servant, for fee and generall poll	0	11	4
Margrat Martine, for fee and generall poll..	0	10	0
James Alles, weaver, and his wife, poll	0	18	0
Robert Clerk, merchant ther (no free stock), and his wife	0	12	0
Elizabeth Cruickshank, his servant, for fee and generall poll is.................	0	10	8
Marjiorie Mackonachie, relict of Thomas Rind, merchant, whose poll would have been £2 10s., poll...	1	2	8
Elspet Rind, her daughter, heires to her father, poll	2	16	0
Jean Inglish, her servant, for fee and generall poll.................................	0	10	8
George Taylor, merchant ther, his poll is £2 10s., (his stock being above 500 merks), *inde*	2	16	0
Item, his wife, and four children *in familia*, poll	1	10	0
Jean Fiddes, servant, for fee and generall poll..	0	11	4
Janet Hunter, his servant, for fee and generall poll.................................	0	9	0
Marjiorie Walker, spouse to George Hector, weaver ther, her poll	0	6	0
James Smith, merchant ther, and his wife, poll.......................................	0	12	0
Isobell Stewart and Christian Couper, his servants, for fee and generall poll ...	1	2	8
William Taylor, servant and œconomus in the Kings Colledge, for fee and generall poll	1	19	4
William Webster, merchant ther (no free stock), and his wife, their poll is......	0	12	0
George Forsyth, shoemaker ther, and his wife, poll.................................	0	18	0
John Robb, taylor ther, and his wife, poll..	0	18	0
Janet Marr, relict of Patrick Norvall, flesher ther, her poll is.....................	0	6	0
And his trading stock being above 500 merks, his poll (if alive) would have been £2 10s., the third part whereof is payable by her, *inde*.............	0	16	8
Katheren Norvall, her daughter, and spouse to James Scot, dragoune, her poll,	0	6	0
Agnes Gibsone, relict of Alexander Watt, glover ther, her poll is	0	6	0
Andrew Robertsone, shoemaker, and his wife	0	18	0
Alexander Grig, wright, and his wife, poll..	0	18	0
John Fides and Alexander Rust, indwellers ther, and their wives, poll	1	4	0
James Watt, cap-maker, and his wife...	0	18	0
Keneth Fraser, measson, and his wife, poll	0	18	0
Alexander Molysone, merchant ther (his free stock being above 500 merks, but not extending to 5000 merks), poll...	2	16	0
Jean Stephan, relict of George Cae, her poll..	0	6	0
Margaret Leitch, relict of William Johnstone, baxter ther, her poll is............	0	6	0
Bessie Clerk, spouse to William Shirres, glover ther, at present ane souldier, her poll is...	0	6	0
Margrat Robertsone, relict of Charles Messer, whose poll (if alive) would have been £4, the third pairt whereof and generall poll is......................	1	12	8
Alexander Annand, cook in the Kings Colledge, and his wife, poll................	0	18	0
John Andersone and James Wilsone, indwellers ther, and their wives, poll......	1	4	0
James Broune, merchant ther, whose stock being above 500 merks, his poll, with his wifes generall poll, is..	3	2	0
Item, two children, James and Margrat Brouns, poll................................	0	12	0

VIII. PRESBYTRIE OF ABERDEEN.

Isobell Lawsone, his servant, for fee and generall poll................................	£0	10	0
John Chalmer, merchant ther (no stock), and his wife................................	0	12	0
William Thomsone, weaver ther, and his wife..	0	18	0
Andrew Gray, elder, couper ther, and his wife..	0	18	0
William Smith, elder and blacksmith, and Agnes Cook, his spouse, poll..........	0	18	0
Issobell Ritchie, servant, for fee and generall poll.....................................	0	9	0
Janet Forsyth, servant, for fee and generall poll.......................................	0	7	4
Alexander Gray and John Arthur, taylors, and their wives, poll....................	1	16	0
Jean Mitchell, servant, for fee and generall poll.......................................	0	9	0
Patrick Fraser ther (no free stock, over and above what he hath mortified to the Kings Colledge), poll for himself and his wife is............................	0	12	0
Methilda Angus, relict of William Mill, bookbinder in Old Aberdeen, her poll,	0	6	0
Item, her daughter, Margrat Mill, poll...	0	6	0
William Taylor, maltman ther, his poll...	0	12	0
David Cristell, wright ther, and his wife and daughter................................	1	4	0
George Simmer, weaver, and his wife, poll..	0	18	0
Helen Gray, his servant, for fee and generall poll......................................	0	10	0
George Mackey and William Moir, taylors, and their wives, their poll............	1	16	0
Item, two servants, each of their fees 4 merks per annum, their poll is............	0	14	8
John Ross, weaver, and his wife, poll is..	0	18	0
Duncan Ross, blacksmith ther, and his wife..	0	18	0
James Lilie, taylor, and his wife, poll..	0	18	0
John Bannerman, fermer ther (no free stock), poll for himself and his wife is	0	12	0
John Ogilvie, his servant, for fee and generall poll....................................	0	12	8
Katheren Andersone, servant for fee and generall poll................................	0	8	8
Margrat Melvine, for fee and generall poll..	0	10	0
John Moir, taylor ther, and his wife and daughter, poll...............................	1	4	0
Elspet Laurenstone, servant, for fee and generall poll................................	0	10	0
Andrew Abell, weaver, and his wife, poll..	0	18	0
Andrew Cuming, shoomaker, and his wife..	0	18	0
Alexander Jellie, shoemaker, and his wife, and an daughter *in familia*, poll......	1	4	0
Patrick Skeen, merchant, and his wife, their free stock being above 500 merks, poll is...	3	2	0
Jean Courage, his servant, for fee and generall poll...................................	0	10	0
John Grig, merchant ther, and his wife, their stock being above 500 merks, poll,	3	2	0
Item, four children, their poll	1	4	0
Item, two servants, each of their fees is £8, *inde* with the generall poll.........	1	0	0
James Fiddes, fermer, his free stock under 5000 merks, poll is	2	16	0
For his wife and six children	2	2	0
James Dugid, his servant, for fee and generall poll....................................	0	14	0
Item, two women servants, for fee and generall poll...................................	1	0	0
Andrew Smith, merchant ther, his free stock being above 500 merks, poll for himself, his wife, and two children...	3	14	0
Jean Mullen, servant, for fee and generall poll..	0	9	0
John Bodell, fermer ther, and his wife, poll	0	12	0
Janet Bodell, servant, for fee and generall poll...	0	10	0

12. TOUNE OF OLD ABERDEEN.

William Sangster, fermer ther, and his wife, and three children *in familia*, poll	£1	10	0
George Leith, servant, for fee and generall poll	0	12	8
Christian Mathewsone, servant, for fee and generall poll	0	10	0
Thomas Andersone, shoemaker, his free stock above 500 merks, poll for himself and his wife is	3	2	0
Item, Elizabeth Andersone, his daughter, poll	0	6	0
Jean Sangster, servant, for fee and generall poll is	0	8	0
James Conquergood, gardener, and his wife, poll	0	18	0
Richard Conquergood, servant, for fee and generall poll	0	8	0
Elizabeth Hervie, servant, for fee and generall poll	0	10	0
Barbra Gray, relict of Alexander Yeats, merchant ther, poll	0	6	0
William Volum, weaver, and his wife, poll	0	18	0
Jean Fidler, servant, for fee and generall poll	0	9	0
Jean Gray, indweller ther, her poll is	0	6	0
George Cristell, wright ther, and his wife, poll	0	18	0
James Auld, mair depute, and his wife, poll	0	12	0
John Auld, mair depute, and his wife, and Elizabeth Auld, his daughter, poll,	0	18	0
William Watt, shoomaker, and his wife, poll	0	18	0
Isobell Chamer, servant, for fee and generall poll	0	9	6
William Robb, weaver, and his wife, poll	0	18	0
James Thomson, younger, merchant, and his wife, poll	0	12	0
Helen Wilsone, servant, for fee and generall poll	0	10	0
Robert Muresone, merchant (no free stock), and his wife, poll	0	12	0
Alexander Simpsone, merchant (no free stock), and his wife, poll	0	12	0
Marjiorie Sled, servant, for fee and generall poll is	0	8	0
Thomas More, merchant ther, and his wife, poll	0	12	0
George Craighead, measson ther, and his wife, poll	0	18	0
Alexander and William Birnes, merchants, their poll	0	12	0
Alexander Gordon, gentleman, and his wife, and daughter *in familia*, poll	3	18	0
Robert Davidson, indweller ther, and his wife, poll	0	12	0
John Nicoll, fermer ther, and his wife, and two children *in familia*, poll	1	4	0
George Henderson, fermer ther, and his wife, poll	0	12	0
William Swape, glover ther, and his wife, poll	0	18	0
William Miller, indweller ther, and his wife, poll	0	12	0
Margrat Fraser, spouse to Thomas Watsone, souldier	0	6	0
Thomas Taylor, merchant ther (no stock), and his wife, poll	0	12	0
Thomas Collie, mair depute, and his wife, and two children, William and Isobell Collies, poll	1	4	0
Janet Wear ther, and her daughter, Anna Harrow	0	12	0
Elizabeth Couts, servant, for fee and generall poll	0	8	8
Isobell Lindsay, widow ther, her poll is	0	6	0
George Adam, advocat ther, and his wife, and two children *in familia*, poll,	5	4	0
Janet Garden, servant, her poll	0	6	0
Janet Glass and Katheren Youngsone, widows, poll	0	12	0
William Andersone and Peter Knight, shoomakers, and their wives, poll	1	16	0
Jean Young, spouse to Thomas Mouat ther, poll	0	6	0

VIII. PRESBYTRIE OF ABERDEEN.

Item, Alexander Leitch and Andrew Aberdein, servants to William Hay, collector (no fees), poll is	£0	12	0
Mary Menzies, relict of Adam Pitendrich, poll	0	6	0
William Thomson, indweller ther, and his wife	0	12	0
John Jaffrey, taylor ther, poll	0	12	0
Jean Fettes, relict of [ ] Young, seaman, poll	0	6	0
Anna Forbes, indweller ther, poll	0	6	0
Alexander Forbes of Easter Migvie, gentleman, and his wife, and two daughters, poll	4	4	0
Alexander Forbes of Haughtone, gentleman, and his wife, and three children, poll	4	10	0
Marjiorie Tause ther, and Margrat Wright, relict of William Forbes ther	0	12	0
John Knight, shoomaker, and his wife, poll	0	18	0
Gilbert Ronaldson, merchant ther (no free stock), and his wife	0	12	0
Isobell Christie, relict of George Broune	0	6	0
James Auld, younger, mair deput, poll	0	6	0
John Mackgie, indweller ther, and his wife, poll	0	12	0
Helen Torie, indweller ther, poll	0	6	0
Robert Mill, bookbinder, and his wife, poll	0	18	0
Marjiorie Mackonachie, servant, for fee and generall poll	0	9	0
John Simpsone, taylor, poll	0	12	0
Patrick Reid, merchant ther (no free stock), and his wife, poll	0	12	0
Agnes Sangster, indweller ther, poll	0	6	0
Jealls Simpsone, relict of George Saint, poll	0	6	0
Anna Irvine, relict of William Chalmer, measson ther, her poll	0	6	0
Margrat Smart, relict of James Arnold, sub-porter in the Kings Colledge, and her son, William, poll	0	12	0
John Barnet, weaver ther, and his wife, poll	0	18	0
John Thomsone, servant, for fee and generall poll	0	9	4
Janet Mill, spouse to Alexander Litlejohn, poll	0	6	0
Agnes Gibsone (not married), poll	0	6	0
Margrat George, relict of John Elmsly, weaver ther, her poll is	0	6	0
Margrat Andersone, relict of William Forbes, taylor, her poll is	0	6	0
James Sandesone, glover, and his wife, poll	0	18	0
Elizabeth Hay, relict of James Mackonachie	0	6	0
William Hendersone, merchant, his stock above 500 merks, poll for himself and his wife, and three children *in familia*,	4	0	0
Margrat Robertsone, servant, for fee and generall poll	0	10	0
Agnes Suape, servant, for fee and generall poll is	0	8	8
Master John Gordon, comissar clerk of Aberdeen, his poll is	6	6	0
Item, Elizabeth Irvine, his wife, and three children	1	4	0
Mr. Francis Irvine, gentleman, *in familia*, poll	3	6	0
Margrat Findlater, Isobell Hay, and Margrat Williamsone, servants, their poll,	1	14	0
Anna Duncan, relict of Mr. Robert Forbes, regent, whose poll would been as a gentleman £3, the third pairt wherof payable by her, and generall poll,	1	6	0
Item, Isobell and Elizabeth, her children, their poll	0	12	0

12. TOUNE OF OLD ABERDEEN.

Janet Davidsone and Jean Simpsone, servants, for fee and generall poll	£1	0	0
Marjorie and Helen Gordons, their poll is	0	12	0
Katheren Ross, relict of John Ross, janitor in the Kings Colledge of Aberdeen, her husbands stock being above 500 merks, and not 5000 merks, her poll	1	2	8
Christian Davidsone and Elspet Wolum, servants, for fee and generall poll is	1	2	8
Mr. Patrick Gordon, humanist in the Kings Colledge of Aberdeen, his poll as a gentleman is	3	6	0
Item, Mr. Thomas Gordon, his son, his poll is	3	6	0
Item, Helen Gordon, his daughter, poll is	0	6	0
George Gibsone, servant, for fee and generall poll is	0	10	0
Jean Hay, servant, for fee and generall poll is	0	9	4
Alexander Gordon, indweller ther, and his wife, he being a gentleman	3	12	0
Two children *in familia*, Hugo and Margrat, poll	0	12	0
Mary Adamsone, servant, for fee and generall poll	0	10	8
Elspet Forbes, relict of William Christie, her poll	0	6	0
Jean More, relict of [ ] Robertson, workman, her poll is	0	6	0
William Scot, mair deput ther, and his wife, poll	0	12	0
Elizabeth and Marjiorie Lindsayes, their poll	0	12	0
Doctor Patrick Urquhart, doctor of medicine in the Kings Colledge, his poll is	12	6	0
Item, his lady, and eight children *in familia*, their poll	2	14	0
Marjiorie Smith, a friend *in familia*, her poll	0	6	0
George Shand, Barbra Nicoll, and Marjiorie Suape, for fee and generall poll is	1	14	0
Master George Skeen, professor of philosophie in the said Colledge, a gentleman, his poll is	3	6	0
Jean Thoris, daughter to the deceast William Thores of Muresk, whose elder brothers poll is £4, the third pairt whereof payable be her, with the generall poll is	1	12	8
James Thores, her brother, his poll is	0	6	0
Anna Abernethie, servant, for fee and generall poll is	0	10	0
May Hog, indweller ther, her poll is	0	6	0
Mary Hay, servant, for fee and generall poll is	0	10	0
John Barclay, merchant in Old Aberdeen, his stock above 500 merks, but not extending to 5000 merks, his poll is	2	16	0
Item, Mr. William Barclay, his brother, and Mistress Jean Barclay, his sister,	0	12	0
Item, Marjiorie Elles, servant, for fee and generall poll is	0	10	0
Marjiorie King, relict of Peter Walace, indweller ther	0	6	0
Balive James Thomson, fermer in Old Aberdeen (no free stock), and his wife,	0	12	0
John Logan, servant, for fee and generall poll is	0	14	0
Alexander Mackie, servant, for fee and generall poll is	0	12	8
Helen Dyce, servant, for fee and generall poll is	0	9	4
Mr. Patrick Walker of Toreleith, his valued rent being above £50, his poll is	4	6	0
Item, his wife and five children, their poll is	1	16	0
(The rest of his familie are polled in New Machar).			
Doctor George Midletone, principall in the Kings Colledge, his poll of a gentleman is	3	6	0

VIII. PRESBYTRIE OF ABERDEEN.

Item, his lady and sex children *in familia*, their poll is	£2	2	0
Jean Catto and Janet Black, each of their fees 16 merks per annum, *inde* of poll	1	2	8
Master William Black, regent in the King's Colledge, his poll as ane gentleman,	3	6	0
Item, his wife, and five children, poll is	1	16	0
James Smith, his servant (no fee), poll	0	6	0
Barbra Logan, servant, for fee and generall poll	0	16	0
Christian Scott and Margrat Lamb, servants, for fee and generall poll	1	2	8
Mr. George Fraser, sub-principal in the Kings Colledge, his poll as a gentleman,	3	6	0
Item, his lady, and five children *in familia*, poll is	1	16	0
Janet Davidson, servant, for fee and generall poll	0	16	0
Marjorie Likley, for fee and generall poll	0	10	8
Patrick Smith, merchant (no stock), and Isobell Stephan, his wife	0	12	0
Jannet Forbes, relict of Mr. George Riccart of Arnadge, her poll, as the third part of her husbands, is	4	6	0
Henreta Seatone, her servant, for fee and generall poll	0	16	0
Janet Shirres and Elspet Stephan, servants, for fee and generall poll	1	3	0
James Bannerman, indweller ther, and his wife, poll	0	12	0
Mr. James Smith, doctor of the Grammar School, he paying as ane gentleman, his poll is	3	6	0
William Gordon his valued rent in New Machar pariochin being above £50, poll for himself, his lady, and five children, is	6	2	0
Margrat Gray, servant, for fee and generall poll is	0	12	0
Janet Farquherson, for fee and generall poll	0	11	4
Agnes Watson, daughter to Alexander Watson, shoemaker	0	6	0
Margrat Philpe, servant to Gilbert Andersone, pentioner, for fee and poll	0	9	0
Jean Henderson, relict of Andrew Cassie of Whitstripes, he being a gentleman, her poll is	1	6	0
Mr. John Robertsone, gentleman (stock under 5000 merks), poll, with the generall poll, is	3	6	0
Item, Helen Shand, his spouse, her generall poll is	0	6	0
Item, Margrat Robertsone, servant, £8 per annum, her poll	0	10	0
William Baxter, indweller in Old Aberdeen (whose free stock is above 500 merks, but does not extend to 5000 merks), his poll, with the generall poll, is	2	16	0
Item, Isobell Bremer, his spouse, her generall poll is	0	6	0
Item, William, John, James, Janet, Agnes, Rachell, and Isobell Baxters, his children, their poll is	2	2	0
Item, David Grigorie, his servant, for fee and generall poll is	0	16	0
Item, George Baxter, alimented *in familia*, his generall poll is	0	6	0
Item, Margrat Hay, servant, for fee and generall poll is	0	10	8
Elizabeth Reid and Elspet Thome, servants, for fee and generall poll	1	2	8
Janet Moir, relict of William Logan, indweller ther, whose poll, if alive (his stock being above 500 merks), would have been £2 10s., the third pairt whereof payable by her, with the generall poll of 6s., is	1	2	8
Item, Isobell Moir, her relatione *in familia*, her generall poll	0	6	0
Item, George M'Allan, her servant, for fee and generall poll	0	16	0

13. TOUNE AND FREEDOM OF ABERDEEN. 595

Item, Janet Wisheart, servant, for fee and generall poll is	£0	11	4
Item, Marjiorie Hendersone, servant, for fee and generall poll	0	10	8
James Knight, merchant ther (his free stock being above 500 merks, but not extending to 5000 merks), his poll, with the generall poll of 6s., is	2	16	0
Item, Janet Low, his spouse, her poll is	0	6	0
Item, James, Arthur, Christian, Elspet, Jean, Anna, Janet, Sarah, and Katheren Knights, his children *in familia*, their poll is	2	14	0
Item, James Smith, servant (no fee), his generall poll is	0	6	0
Item, Agnes Gray and Elspet Sympsone, servants, for fee and generall poll	0	19	0
Item, ane other woman servant, for fee and generall poll	0	9	6
Item, Arthur Knight, shoemaker ther, and his wife, poll	0	18	0
Item, James Walker, indweller ther (no trade, no free stock), and Christian Muir, his spouse, their poll is	0	12	0
Item, Margrat Couper, relict of William Orem, indweller in Old Aberdeen (no free stock), and a son of age, called William Orem, their poll is	0	12	0
Item, Janet Clerk, servant, fee 14 merks, fortieth pairt and generall poll is	0	10	8
Item, Isobell Still, servant, the like fee and poll	0	10	8
Item, Janet Irving, servant, fee £8, fortieth pairt and generall poll is	0	10	0
	£475	6	2
Summa of the Toune of OLD ABERDEEN is	£475	6	2

OLD MACHAR AND OLD ABERDEEN

NAME (both sexes)	Page	NAME (both sexes)	Page
ABELL Andrew	575(2)	ARBUTHNOT Christian	564
ABERDEEN Andrew	590	ARBUTHNOTT Isobell	564
George	575,587	ARCHIE Margarat	566(2)
Peter	576	ARDES John	567
ABERDEIN Andrew	592	ARNOLD James	592
ABERDOUR James	575	Margrat	592
ABERNETHIE Anna	593	William	592
Peter	573	ARTHUR Alexander	564
ADAM Alexander	553	John	590
Andrew	585	AULD Elizabeth	591
Donald	560,561	James	591,592
George	591	John	556,591
Jean	561		
Margarat	564	**BADENSCOTH** Laird of	564
Thomas	584	BAIN Margaret	561
ADAMSONE Mary	593	BALGOUNIE Laird of	554(3),555
AIDIE William	571	BANNERMAN Alexander	576
AIKEN John	569	James	594
ALDMAN Janet	586	John	556,590
ALLAN Alexander	558	BARBER George	584
Elizabeth	586	BARCLAY Jean	593
George	556,566,587	John	593
Jannet	564	William	593
Margarat	564	BARNET Barbara	572
ALLES James	589	John	565,592
ANDERSON Alexander	585	BARRON John	555
Gilbert	571	Margarat	555
James	564	BARTLET Andrew	561
Margrat	585,587	George	557(2),558
Marjiorie	564		559,560
William	584,585,587	Isobell	586
ANDERSONE Agnes	585	James	559
Alexander	567	Margarat	561
Bessie	586	William	560(2),567
Christian	559	BAVERLY James	575
David	557,559	BAXTER Agnes	594
Elizabeth	591	Andrew	557,588
Elspet	586	George	594
Gilbert	594	Isobell	594(2)
Helen	563	James	594
Isobell	567	Janet	594
James	567	John	594
Jannet	568	Rachell	594
Jean	565	William	556,594(2
John	589	BEAVERLY Margrat	588
Katheren	590	BENNET William	575
Margarat	553	BENZIE Jannet	566
Margaret	554	BEVERLEY William	588
Margrat	592	BEVERLY Agnes	583
Thomas	591	Elizabeth	555
William	553,554,565	Elspet	575
	568,572,591	Isobell	568
ANGUS Janet	586	William	568
Margrat	586	BIRNE Alexander	591
Methilda	590	William	591
William	586	BISSET Gilbert	559
ANNAND	564	John	587
Alexander	589	Margrat	587
Jannet	564	BLACK Anna	575

OLD MACHAR AND OLD ABERDEEN

NAME (both sexes)	Page	NAME (both sexes)	Page
B	552	CAIRNGILL Bessie	555
Gilbert	566	CARNGILL Jean	585
James	586	CASSIE Andrew	552,557
Janet	594		594
Margaret	555	Duncan	556,574,589
William	568,575,594	Elizabeth	574
BLACKALL Christian	567	Jannet	574
BLAIR Christian	555	Jean	594
John	553,555	Margarat	574
BLAK B	574	Thomas	574
BLENSHELL Elizabeth	561	CATANACH Elizabeth	560
John	560,561	Margarat	560
Thomas	561	William	560(2)
BODDELL Robert	576	CATTANACH Helen	585
BODELL Janet	590	CATTO Elizabeth	584
John	590	Helen	569
BODIE Elizabeth	554	Jean	594
James	554	William	560
John	552,564	CHALMER Agnes	585
BODWEEL John	557	Alexander	571,572
BOOTH Agnes	554	Anna	592
Alexander	564	Bessie	571
Christian	554	Cloria	563
James	554	Isobell	564(2)
Jean	554(2),564	James	571,572
William	554	Jean	584
BREBNER Anna	563	John	556,565(2)
Catherine	570		590
BRECK George	584	Laury	563
BREMER Isobell	594	Robert	571,575(2)
BRODIE Bessie	555	William	562,564(2)
BROUN Gilbert	556		571,572,592
Jannet	567	CHALMERS Jean	561
Margrat	589	CHAMER Isobell	591
BROUNE George	592	CHAPMAN Elizabeth	559
Gilbert	588	CHARLES Andrew	587
Isobell	592	Elisabeth	563
James	589(2)	CHEYNE Elizabeth	586
BROW Alexander	562,564	Jean	584
Bessie	572	Patrick	584
George	553,563	Peter	556
Jannet	575	CHRISTALL David	572
Margarat	572	CHRISTELL Alexander	555,586
William	572	Elizabeth	555
BROWN Alexander	572,573	Girsell	562
Bessie	565	James	553,554
Marjiorie	560	Jannet	555,558
William	569	John	584
BRUICE Alexander	584	Margrat	584
William	570	CHRISTIE Alexander	556,583
BUCHAN Thomas	585	Elspet	588,593
BULFRIT Robert	567	Isobell	592
BULLFOORD Cloria	583	James	588
BURGES Christian	568	John	559
BURN Alexander	569	Patrick	559,569
		Peter	557
CAE George	589	William	593
Jean	589	CHYNE Alexander	560
CAIE George	565	Andrew	558

OLD MACHAR AND OLD ABERDEEN

NAME (both sexes)	Page	NAME (both sexes)	Page
John	568	George	586
Margarat	555	Isobell	574
Marjiore	568	William	584,587
CLERK Bessie	589	CUIE Margrat	586
Gilbert	576	CULLEN James	588
Isobell	555	Margrat	588
Janet	595	CUMING	586
Jean	576	Andrew	590
John	576	George	584
Robert	589	Sara	583
William	566,567	William	587
COBAN William	569	CUMMING Elspet	588
COLLACE Isobell	585	CUSHNEY George	556
Katheren	585	CUSHNIE Barbra	568
Robert	585	George	568
COLLIE Isobell	591		
Thomas	591	**DANIELL** John	584
William	591	DARG Alexander	553(2)
CONAN George	565	DARGE John	588
CONQUERGOOD James	591	Katheren	588
Richard	591	DAVIDSON Alexander	552,561
COOK Agnes	590		562
COOKE Robert	587	Christian	573
COUPER Agnes	584	Isobell	576
Alexander	584	James	576
Christian	589	Janet	594
Janet	561	Margrat	587
John	584	Marjorie	566
Margarat	553,556	Robert	591
Margrat	584,595	DAVIDSONE Agnes	566
Marjiorie	585	Christian	593
Marjorie	584	George	566,572,573
William	560	Helen	586
COURAGE Jean	590	Isobell	565,566
COUTS Elizabeth	591	James	573(2)
James	576	Janet	593
Robert	570	Jean	561
COW John	570	John	561
COWPER John	587	Margarat	555
CRAIG Alexander	558,573	Marjorie	576
Robert	573	Patrick	565,576
William	564	DEANS Jean	588
CRAIGHEAD Agnes	563	DEINS Agnes	587
Arthur	563	DEY Alexander	576
George	591	John	586
Isobell	571	DICKIE James	585
CRAIGHEADE Andrew	585	DIN Robert	574(2)
CRAWFOORD Besse	563	DIVERTY James	562,563,588
Elizabeth	561	William	563
CREVIE Jannet	564	DOLLAS John	570
John	564	DOUNIE Peter	560
CRISTELL David	590	DOUR Helen	585
Elizabeth	566	DOWNIE John	576
George	591	DRUM Agnes	559
Patrick	566	Bessie	555
CROMBIE William	586	Margarat	574
CRUICKSHANK Barbra	586	Richard	552,555,574
Elisabeth	588	Robert	586
Elizabeth	589	William	568

OLD MACHAR AND OLD ABERDEEN

NAME (both sexes)	Page	NAME (both sexes)	Page
DRUME James	573,574	Christian	564,565
DUGAT John	574	Elizabeth	565,592
DUGID James	590	Elspet	593
DUGUID James	587	Griger	570
William	560	Isobell	592
DUN Mary	564	James	560
DUNBARR Margarat	576	Jannet	594
DUNCAN Anna	557,592	Jean	565(2)
Christian	571	Margrat	592(2)
Elizabeth	570	Marjorie	563
Isobell	561	Robert	586,587,592
Janet	574	Thomas	565(4)
John	569		572,573
Robert	570	Walter	560,561
William	568	William	592(2)
DYCE Agnes	567	FORSYTH Alexander	564
Andrew	584	Andrew	563
Helen	593	Anna	561
Isobell	555,563	Christian	588
		George	562(2),563
ELLES John	584		564,567,589
Marjiorie	593	Janet	590
William	587	Marjiorie	585,588
ELMSLY John	585,592	Thomas	562,563(2)
Margarat	592		567
Margrat	588	FOTHRINGAME John	576
Marie	587	FOTHRINGHAME Marjorie	576
ELPHINSTONE Robert	584	FOULER Christian	561
ELRICK Alexander	554	FRASER Agnes	570
		Alexander	557,583
FALCONER Elizabeth	558	George	594
Peter	586	James	561,585
FARQUARSONE Agnes	561	John	587
James	561	Keneth	589
FARQUERSON Janet	594	Margrat	591
FERGUSON Alexander	566,567	Marjiorie	587
	585	Patrick	590
John	565,585	Peter	556
Margarat	554	William	573
FERGUSONE John	554	FRASSER Christian	555
FETTES Jean	592	FREEMAN John	561
John	557,558	Marjiorie	561
FIDDES James	556,590	FROST Anna	553
Jean	589	Margarat	554
FIDES John	589	FULLER Elizabeth	575
FIDLER Jean	591	George	575
FIFE Patrick	585	FYFE George	571
FIFFE Janet	584	Jean	561
FINDLATER Margrat	592		
William	575(2)	**GAE** Elizabeth	559
FINDLAY James	560	GARDEN Dr.	557
Margarat	553	James Dr.	587
FINNIE Alexander	555,563	Janet	591
Barbra	586	GARIOCH George	585
Elizabeth	555,559	GEDDES Jannet	573
James	559	Mary	566
FORBES Alexander	564,565	GEORGE Margrat	592
	592(2)	GERARD Elizabeth	555
Anna	557,592(2)	GIBB George	564

OLD MACHAR AND OLD ABERDEEN

NAME (both sexes)	Page	NAME (both sexes)	Page
John	575	James	552(3),553,568
GIBSON Alexander	552	Jean	591
Jean	554,565	John	552,553(3)
Katherine	572		554,588
Thomas	565	Margaret	553
GIBSONE Agnes	589,592	Margrat	564,594
Alexander	553	Patrick	555
George	593	Robert	552,554,572
Helen	586	William	554,584,588
Isobell	554	GREIG Alexander	568
James	586	John	568,572
Jannet	568	GRHAME James	563
Margrat	585	GRIG Alexander	589
Robert	554	Elisabeth	555
GILL Agnes	562	George	572
Alexander	553,554	John	572,590
	562(2)	GRIGORIE David	594
Barbara	572	GRUER David	586
Edward	571,572	GUTHRIE Alexander	575
Isobell	554(2)		
Janet	565	**HADDON** Andrew	570
Katherine	562	George	570
William	572	HALL Agnes	576
GLASS Alexander	556,587	Andrew	576
Janet	591	HARROW Anna	591
GLENNIE Christian	571	David	560
Lucres	556,566,567	HARVIE Helen	563
	587	William	562,563(2)
GODSMAN Andrew	561	HAT George	583
GORDON Alexander	557,591,593	William	583
Elisabeth	588	HATT Agnes	583
Elizabeth	569,592	Alexander	553,583
George	586	HAY Elizabeth	592
Helen	593(2)	Isobell	592
Hugo	593	James	560,575
James	562,563(4)	Jean	565,593
	564,571,586	Margrat	594
Janet	585	Mary	593
Jannet	572	William	592
Jean	587	HECTOR George	589
John	552,571,592	Jannet	558
Katheren	586	John	558
Lues	586	Margarat	555,558
Margarat	564	Marjiorie	589
Margrat	588,593	Thomas	555
Marjorie	563,593	HENDERSON George	556,591
Mary	564	Jean	594
Patrick	593	HENDERSONE Alexander	565
Thomas	593		554
William	588,594	Isobell	565
GORDONE James	552(2)	James	554
GRANT Isobell	584	Janet	565
GRAY Agnes	553,595	Jannet	554
Alexander	590	Marjiorie	595
Andrew	584,590	Patrick	565
Barbra	591	William	592
Christian	554	HENDRIE Alexander	569,573,574
Helen	590		576
Isobell	554,564,588	James	573,574

OLD MACHAR AND OLD ABERDEEN

NAME (both sexes)	Page	NAME (both sexes)	Page
John	565,568	JAMESONE Issobell	559
Marjiorie	576	Jane	569
Thomas	559	JEANS Adam	558
HERVIE Alexander	587	Elspeth	558
Elizabeth	591	Isobell	588
James	583	John	572
William	565	William	556,588
HILL Alexander	583	JELLIE Alexander	590
David	557	JOHNS Elspet	586
James	569,570	Margrat	586
Margrat	588	JOHNSTON William	552.571(2)
Marjorie	584	JOHNSTONE Isobell	563
HILTO(W)N Laird of	552,567(2)	James	562,575,585
	568	John	587
HIRD George	566,567	Margaret	589
HOG May	593	William	563,589
HOGG Jean	564	JOSSE Elspeth	553
HUISONE Christian	555	William	553
HUNTER Anna	587		
George	587	**KEITH** Andrew	576
Janet	589	Elizabeth	576
Jean	585	Isobell	554
Margarat	587	Jean	576
HUTCHEON Jean	560,561	Margarat	566
John	561	William	573
		KILGOUR William	566,567
INGLIS Jannet	564(2)	KILLGOUR Jean	567
John	564	Peter	567
William	564	KILLGOURE Bessie	586
INGLISH Jean	589	George	586
Marjiorie	589	KINARD John	587
INGLISS Margrat	585	KING John	584
INNES Agnes	561,565,566	Marjiorie	593
Bessie	586	Patrick	584
Elizabeth	555	KINNAIRD John	556
Jean	554,555	KNIGHT Anna	595
John	555	Arthur	595(2)
Jonn	576	Christian	595
William	573,574,587	Elspet	595
IRONSYD Isobell	564	James	583,595(2)
IRONSYDE James	588	Janet	554,595(2)
IRVING	571	Jean	595
IRVINE Anna	592	John	592
Elizabeth	592	Katheren	595
Francis	592	Peter	591
IRVING Francis	562,563	Sarah	595
Janet	595	KNOUES Margrat	585
Marjiorie	587		
		LAING George	568,588
JACKSON Peter	562	James	584
JACKSONE Jean	566	Marjiorie	561
Margaret	554	LAMB Margrat	594
JAFFRAY Alexander	586	LAURENSTON Margarat	563
James	556,586	LAURENSTONE Barbara	572
Margaret	558	Elspet	590
JAFFREY Elspet	586	John	554,562
John	586,592	LAWRENSONE John	584
JAMESON Andrew	586	LAWSON Isobell	588
George	568	LAWSONE Isobell	590

OLD MACHAR AND OLD ABERDEEN

NAME (both sexes)	Page	NAME (both sexes)	Page
LEAPER Isobell	576	Margarat	570
LEASK John	584(2)	Peter	570
Marjiorie	572	MackGIE John	592
William	584	McGRIGOR Elspeth	570
LEED Elizabeth	554	McINTOSH Janet	558
LEITCH Alexander	592	McKAIN Margarat	553
Margaret	589	MacKEY George	590
LEITH George	585,591	MacKONACHIE Elizabeth	592
Helen	585	James	592
LEONARD Isobell	573	Marjiorie	589,592
LESLIE Alexander	554	McKONEISTON Margarat	570
George	564,573(2)	McPHERSON Elizabeth	572
James	570(2)	MACKIE Agnes	558
Janet	554	Alexander	557,559
John	573,587	Christian	588
Margarat	554,570	Cloria	569
LESLY Margrat	588	John	557,559
LESSLIE John	552	Peter	558
LIGERTWOOD John	571	William	556,576,588
LIKLEY Marjorie	594	MAIN Marjiorie	576
LILIE James	590	MAITLAND Elizabeth	571
LIND Margaret	556	MARISCHALL Margrat	584
LINDSAY Isobell	591	MARNOCH James	556,566,567
LINDSAYE Elizabeth	593		574,588
Marjiorie	593	John	584
LINTON James	569	Lucres	587
LINTONE Alexander	588	William	587
LITLEJOHN Alexander	592	MARR Janet	589
Janet	592	John	572,573
LITTLEJOHN George	553	MARTINE Margrat	589
James	555,588	MASSIE Alexander	572
William	553	Andrew	552,568,587
LOGAN Barbra	568,594	Barbara	568
Janet	594	George	585
John	593	Katherine	572
William	594	Margarat	565
LOGIE Anna	584	Thomas	566
Margaret	558	MATHEWSON Alexander	556
William	558(2)	Isobell	588
LONDIE James	555	James	584
LOVIE Anna	584	MATHEWSONE Alexander	587
George	584	Christian	591
John	585	MEASSON James	585
Margaret	584	MEASSONE George	554
LOW Janet	595	MELVELL John	556
Margrat	587	MELVIN Isobell	568
LOWE Robert	585	John	568(2)
LOWELY Anthony	571	MELVINE Margrat	590
LUCKIE John	570	MENZIES Jean	560(2)
LUNDIE Alexander	588	Margarat	560
John	588	Margaret	553
Margrat	588	Marjore	560
Mariorie	588	Mary	560,592
LYES Alexander	576	Robert	560
		Thomas	558
McALLAN George	594	William	560
McCASTELL James	584	MERSER Isobell	573
McCONACHIE Besse	570	John	572,573
David	570	MESSER Charles	589

OLD MACHAR AND OLD ABERDEEN

NAME (both sexes)	Page	NAME (both sexes)	Page
Margrat	589	Thomas	591
MESSON James	566,567	MORISONE James	565
Jannet	555	Margarat	565
Marjorie	563	Thomas	565
MESSONE George	563	MORTIMER George	558
Isobell	563	Isobell	558
James	556	MORTOUN Elizabeth	558
MIDLETON Alexander	588	MOUAT Jean	591
MIDLETONE George Dr	557,593	Thomas	591
MILL Agnes	563	MOWAT Jannet	564
Elizabeth	560	Thomas	566
George	556,584	MUIR Christian	595
Isobell	568	MULLEN Jean	590
James	556,576,585	MUNDY Isobell	553
Janet	592	MUNZIE Agnas	576
Jean	553,568	Alexander	576
John	553,555,564	James	560
	575,584	MURDO William	563
Margarat	553	MURESONE Robert	591
Margaret	587	MURGAN William	568
Margrat	587,590	MURISON Christian	586
Methilda	590	Jean	586
Robert	592	MURISONE Alexander	588
William	590	MURRAY David	563,585
MILLER William	591	Isobell	567
MILLS Christian	573	John	557,559,565
MILNE Elizabeth	565	Margaret	561
MITCHELL Agnas	569	William	555,586
Agnes	574	MUSKIE Isobell	588
Andrew	561		
Anna	587	**NAIRN** David	574
George	588	James	570
Isobell	588	NAIRNE Agnes	587
Janet	586	David	587
Jean	590	NICOL David	588
John	553,557,559	John	556
Katheren	588	NICOLL Alexander	568
Marjorie	572	Andrew	568
Thomas	586	Barbra	593
William	569,570	David	568
	572(2)	James	561,573
MOIR Dr	571		574,584
Alexander	571	Jean	568
Bessie	571(2)	John	591
Elizabeth	571	Katherine	562
Isobell	594	Marjiorie	568
James	571	Norman	557
Janet	594	William	558,587
Jannet	556	NORVALL Janet	589
John	552,575,590	Katheren	589
Margarat	564	Patrick	589
William	552,564,569		
	587,590	**OGILVIE** John	590
MOLYSONE Alexander	589	OLIPHANT Christian	559
MONTGOMRIE William	588	John	559
MOOR James	584	OREM Margrat	595
MORE Doctor	552	William	595(2)
Christian	584		
Jean	593	**PANMUIRE** Earl of	552,565

OLD MACHAR AND OLD ABERDEEN

NAME (both sexes)	Page	NAME (both sexes)	Page
PATERSONE Elspet	583	William	591
Isobell	588	ROBERTSON	593
PAT(T)ON Anna	557	Alexander	562,564
George	552,557(2)	Anna	584
James	557	James	571
Janet	557	Jean	593
John	557	Margarat	564
Katherin	557	William	567,575(2)
Margarat	557		586
PAULL Alexander	554	ROBERTSONE Agnes	554
Anna	563	Andrew	553,554
James	563		570,589
PEACO(C)K George	552,572,573	Besse	570
PEDDOR John	557(2)	Christian	567
PETER Alexander	570	Elizabeth	560
Jean	570	George	569,570,585
PETRIE Jannet	565	Girsell	562
PHILP Agnes	570	Helen	594
Elspeth	558	Isobell	572
James	570	James	562,567,585
PHILPE Margrat	594	John	552,570
PIRIE Robert	567		583,594
PIRY Mary	567	Margarat	561,571
PITENDRICH Adam	592	Margrat	589,592
	573		594
Mary	592	Thomas	559,567
PROCTER Barbara	564	William	552,557
Robert	564	ROBSON Bessie	568
PROCTOR Alexander	555	ROGIE Agnes	585
Bessie	555	Euphemia	561
Christian	554	RONALD George	556,585
George	554	Jean	585
Jean	555	RONALDSON Gilbert	592
William	562,563	ROSS Donald	586
PYET Alexander	575	Duncan	590
		Janet	587
RAE Robert	561	John	587,590,593
RAFF Archibald	575	Katheren	593
REID Elizabeth	594	Robert	588
James	567	RUSSELL William	560
Jean	565	RUST Alexander	589
John	559	Isobell	563
Patrick	592		
RENIE William	564	SAINT George	592
RICCART George	594	Jealls	592
Jannet	594	SANDESONE James	592
RIND Elspet	589	SANDILANDS George	566
Marjiorie	589	Jean	566
Thomas	589	Magdalen	566
RITCHIE Andrew	572	Marjorie	566
Elizabeth	575	Rachell	566
Hector	557,558,559	Patrick	552,566(4)
Isobell	553,559,571	William	566
Issobell	590	SANGSTER Agnes	592
Jean	558	Alexander	556,557
John	554(2),584		559
Peter	557	Andrew	557,559
William	571,585	Cloria	563
ROBB John	589	Jean	585,591

OLD MACHAR AND OLD ABERDEEN

NAME (both sexes)	Page	NAME (both sexes)	Page
John	584	Janet	586
William	556,559	Jean	561,564,565
	569,591	John	562,564(2)
SCLAIT Marjorie	555		566,584
Robert	555	Marjiorie	593
SCOT James	589	Marjorie	555
Katheren	589	Patrick	594
William	593	Robert	565,566
SCOTT Barbara	566	Thomas	584
Christian	594	William	585,588,590
Isobell	566	SPARK Margarat	561
SCOUGALL John	563	STEINSONE Barbra	586
Margaret	563	Christian	554
SETON(E) Henreta	594	STEPHAN Elspet	594
John	569(2)	Isobell	594
SHAND Agnes	554	Jean	589
George	593	STEVEN Alexander	567
Helen	594	Bessie	554
Robert	587	Isobell	554
Thomas	555	James	554
SHEEPHERD James	560	Robert	558
William	575	STEWART Elspet	587
SHIRRES Bessie	589	Isobell	589
Janet	594	John	587
Thomas	587	STILL Alexander	552(2),553(2)
William	589		554
SIMER Christian	585	Andrew	576
Marjorie	586	Christane	553
SIMMER George	590	Christian	588
SIMPSONE Alexander	575,591	Darg	553
Janet	585	David	558
Jealls	592	Elspet	588
Jean	593	George	558,573,574
John	592	Isobell	553,554
SINCLAR Elizabeth	587		555,595
SINCLAIR Robert	584	James	557,558
SINIER Margrat	587		573,574
SKEEN Bessie	567	Janet	555
George	593	Jean	553
Isobell	588	John	563,564
James	576		569(2)
John	576	Robert	572
Margrat	588	Thomas	552,555,557
Patrick	590		559,568
Robert	567	STOTT James	554
SKINNER George	560	Peter	568
SLED Marjorie	591	STRACHAN Alexander	556,583
SLIDDERS John	585	John	570
SMART Margrat	592	Margarat	555
Robert	568	STROGS Isobell	565
SMITH Adam	564	John	565
Agnes	565,566,590	SUAPE Agnes	592
Andrew	590	Marjiorie	593
Christian	564,588	SUMMER Jean	565
Elizabeth	572	John	575
Isobell	594	SWAPE William	591
James	557,560,561	SWAPS Thomas	587
	589,594(2)	SYME Margart	555
	595	SYMER Jannet	555

OLD MACHAR AND OLD ABERDEEN

NAME (both sexes)	Page	NAME (both sexes)	Page
SYMMER William	553	TURRIFFE James	583
SYMPSONE Elspet	595		
George	558	**UMPHRA** Thomas	588
		UMPHREY Jean	554
TAIT Alexander	566	John	554
TAUSE Marjiorie	592	Margarat	554
TAYLOR Alexander	559,566(2)	URQUHART Patrick Dr	593
George	556,586,589		
Isobell	564	**VOLUM** William	591
James	558		
Jane	558	**WACHOP** Jean	560(2)
Jannet	564	WALACE Marjiorie	593
John	569	Peter	593
Marjiroie	585	WALKER Alexander	557,558
Thomas	562,564,591	Barbara	554
William	562,564	Christian	564,595
	589,590	George	561,564
THAIN Jean	553	James	595
THOM Elspet	588	Jean	585,586
THOME Elspet	594	John	586
George	588	Margarat	553
Helen	588	Marjiorie	561,589
THOMSON James	591	Marjorie	572
James	593	Patrick	593
Katherine	588	Robert	564
Thomas	583	William	564,572,573
William	592	WATSON Adam	553
THOMSONE Agnes	553	Agnes	568,594
Bessie	584	Alexander	559,594
Christian	585	Christian	553
James	556,574	George	559
John	592	John	586
Peter	564	WATSONE Alexander	557,586
Robert	571	Barbara	564
William	557,558,560	Christane	553
	574,576,587	Christian	555
	590	Edward	574
		Isobell	575
THORES James	593	Jean	558
William	593	Margrat	591
THORIS Jean	593	Thomas	591
THOW Jean	555	WATT Agnes	584,589
TILLERY Elizabeth	562	Alexander	589
George	553	Elizabeth	554
Jean	565	James	558,589
John	553	Jean	574
Thomas	565	John	554
TILLIRY Alexander	571,572	Margaret	555
Thomas	564	Marjiorie	585
TORIE Helen	592	Thomas	557,558(2)
TOUCH George	560	William	560,585,591
TOUGH Jean	560	WEAR Janet	591
TOUKS James	570	WEBSTER Alexander	576
TROUP Alexander	563,564	David	576
	569(3),573	Elspet	585
Elisabeth	573	Isobell	565
James	569	James	576
Jean	564	Jannet	576
Marjiorie	561,564	Margarat	561
William	573(2)		

OLD MACHAR AND OLD ABERDEEN

NAME (both sexes)	Page	NAME (both sexes)	Page
William	561,589	Thomas	562
WILLIAMSONE Margrat	592	WOLUM Elspet	593
WILSONE Andrew	557,559	WRIGHT Agnes	554
Bessie	568	Margrat	592
Helen	591		
Isobell	588	**YAITT** James	568
James	572,589	YEATS Alexander	591
Jean	585	Barbra	591
Robert	588	YEATT Alexander	583
William	556,568,586	YETT Alexander	554
WISHEART Agnes	562	Jannet	558
Alexander	568	YOUNG	592
Elizabeth	560	Jean	591,592
Isobell	562	John	568
James	562(3)	YOUNGSONE Isobell	573
Janet	595	Katheren	591
Jean	567	Patrick	572,573
John	586	William	573
Robert	563		

OLD MACHAR AND OLD ABERDEEN

PLACE NAME	Page	PLACE NAME	Page
ABERDEEN (NEW)	555(2), 557(2), 562 573, 574, 592	KEYSTON(E) KINGS COLLEDGE	569(2) 55, 587, 588(2)
ARIBURN	567		589(2), 590, 592
ARNADGE	594		593(5), 594(2)
BADENSCOTH	564	LINKS	563, 569(3)
BALGOUNIE	552(2), 553(2) 554(4), 555	LOANHEAD	560, 561
BALHELVIE	566	MENDURNO	565(3), 566(2)
BARNNES	575	MERNES/SHIRE	571
BELTIE	571	MIGVIE, Easter	592
BERRIHILL	552, 561(3)	MURCAR	552, 553
BODACHRA	568	MURESK	593
BRIDGETOUNE/BRIGTOUN	557, 559		
BUCKIE	557,559	NEWHILLS	568
		NEWMACHAR	568, 593, 594
CABERSTON	576	NORTH LEITH	555
CAIRNFIELD	552, 555		
CASSIE-END	572	OLD ABERDEEN	552, 555, 556, 557(3), 566
CATHOK MILL	555		567, 568, 569, 571, 574(3)
CLARKSHILL/CLERKHILL	557, 559		575, 583(2), 584(2), 585(3)
COLLEDGE BOUNDS	583, 584(2), 585(3) 586,587		586(2), 587(2), 588, 590 593(2), 594, 595
COTTON(E)	552, 566(4), 588	OLD MACHAR	552
CULSALMOND	562		
		PANMUIRE	552, 565
DENFIELD/DENSFIELD	557, 559(2)	PERSLEY/PERSLIE	557, 558(2)
DENSTOUN(E)	557, 558	PERVVINES	568
DON	552(3), 561(2), 562 563, 568, 571(2)	PETERSTON(E)/PETERSTOUN PITMUXTON	552, 575 552, 572(2), 573(2)
DYCE	555		
		ROTHEMAY	586
EDINBURGH	563, 569	RUTHRESTOWN/RUTHRESTONE	552, 561(2)
FROSTERHILL	576	SCOTSTON/SCOTSTOUN SEATON(E)/SEATOUN(E)	571(4) 552, 562, 563(2)
GALLOWGAIT PORT	569		571, 574
GILCOMSTO(U)NE	552, 559, 560(7), 561	SILVERBURNE	554
GLENCARVIE	586	SPITTALL/SPITTEL(L)	569(2), 570, 575
GORDONS MILL	566, 567	STANKYAIRD	575(2)
GRAMMAR SCHOOL	594	SUNISYDE	552, 575(4)
GRANDHOM	552, 557(4), 558(2)		
		TARBOTHILL	565(2)
HARDGATE	573	TILLEDRON	566
HAUGHTONE	592	TORELEITH	593
HILLHEAD/HILLHEID	556, 567		
HILLTO(W)N	552, 567(4), 568(3)	WA(L)KMILL	566, 567
HOSPITAL/OLD ABERDEEN	555	WASTFIELD/WESTFIELD	552, 555
		WHYTESTRYPES/WHYTSTRYPS/	552, 573(3)
JUSTICE MILLS	576	WHITSTRIPES	574, 594

OLD MACHAR AND OLD ABERDEEN

OCCUPATIONS

ADVOCAT	1	MAIR DEPUTE	5
		MALTMAN	7
BAILIE	2	MASTER	
" """	1	Musicle School	1
BALIVE	1	MEASSON/MESSON	9
BAXTER	2	MERCHANT	42
BELT WEAVER	1	MILLERT	3
BIBLIOTHICARIAN	1	MINISTER	1
BLACKSMITH	5		
BOOKBINDER	3	NOTTAR	1
CAPER	1	OECONOMUS	1
CAPPMAKER	1		
CHURCH BEDDALL	1	PENTIONER	2
CLERK	2	PRENTICE	2
COLLECTOR	3	PRINCIPALL	
COMISSAR CLERK	1	Kings Colledge	1
COMMISSIONER	4	PROFESSOR	
COOK	1	Divinty	1
COPPERSMITH	1	Philosophie	1
COUPER	3		
		REGENT	3
DOCTOR			
Grammar School	1	SADDLER	1
Medicine	3	SEAMAN	1
DRAGOUNE	1	SERVANT	
		Female	150
FARMER/FERMER	63	Male	94
FISHER	2	Unspec.	7
FLESHER	11	SHOEMAKER	57
		SMITH	5
GARDNER	3	SOULDIER	2
GENTLEMAN	19	SUB-PRINCIPALL	
GLOVER	5	Kings Colledge	1
GLOWER	1	SUB-PORTER	1
GRASSMAN	5		
GRASSWOMAN	2	TAYLOR	29
GUNSMITH	2	THESAURER	1
HUMANIST	2	WAKSTER/WAXTER	2
		WEAVER/WYVER	51
INDWELLER	60	WHEELWRIGHT	2
		WORKMAN	9
JANITOR	2	WRIGHT	9
LITSTER	2		